AF870878

The Dopamine Debt

Verses Kindler Publication

Verses Kindler Publication.

Website: www.verseskindlerpublication.com

The Dopamine Debt

By: Mr. Anshu Varma

ISBN: 978-81-69248-14-3

1st Edition

Price: INR 299/$15.00

Disclaimer

The Dopamine Debt is authored by Anshu Varma. The entirety of this published work comprises the original content of the author, who has undertaken diligent efforts in its editing. The characters depicted herein may be fictitious or inspired by real events; however, they are not intended to cause offense or represent any prejudice against any caste or system. Any similarity to the names of actual individuals, locations, or institutions is purely coincidental and serves the narrative. The author bears sole responsibility for the originality of this work; the publisher assumes no liability thereof.

Table of Contents

Preface 1

Chapter 1 - The First Hit 8

Chapter 2 - Pleasure Without Purpose 19

Chapter 3 – The Dopamine Debt 33

Chapter 4 — Reels, Swipes, and Synthetic Validation 51

Chapter 5 — Desire, Direction, and Energy 65

Chapter 6 — The Trap Phase 80

Chapter 7 — The Guilt Loop 93

Chapter 8 — Motivation Fatigue 103

CHAPTER 9 - The Silent Struggle 113

Chapter 10 — When Coping Becomes Identity 124

Chapter 11 - Why Detox Fails 133

Chapter 12 — Friction as Medicine 143

Chapter 13 — The Reset Protocol 153

Chapter 14 — Relearning Focus 164

Chapter 15 — Discipline Without Harshness 177

Chapter 16 — From Stimulation to Direction 185

Conclusion 190

Preface

This Book Is Not Here to Save You

This book is not here to rescue you from your habits or manufacture a dramatic turning point. It does not promise discipline, motivation, or transformation on a fixed schedule.

It also does not frame your struggle as a moral failure, a lack of ambition, or a defect of character. Those explanations are familiar to most people, and they rarely lead to anything useful.

This book begins from a quieter assumption. Something in your life has been feeling a little out of alignment for some time.

Most readers will recognize themselves in what follows, even if they have not articulated it clearly before. They are aware of the frequency of their involuntary phone grabs.

They notice how easily time dissolves into scrolling, clicking, watching, and switching.

They sense how difficult it has become to sustain attention, even on things that matter to them. Work feels heavier than it used to. Rest feels less restorative. Joy comes swiftly and departs so swiftly.

Nothing appears remarkable enough to cause concern, yet nothing appears stable enough to be ignored. Short-form content, dating apps, social media, and pornography are not cultural coincidences.

They are systems built to reward immediacy, novelty, and emotional relief with minimal cost.

When exposure to such systems becomes constant, something subtle begins to shift. What once felt engaging loses its pull, and waiting starts to feel uncomfortable. Attention scatters more easily, and stillness becomes harder to tolerate.

What once required effort now feels unnecessary, and what requires effort begins to feel strangely unrewarding.

This shift happens quietly. There is no clear moment where things break. Life continues to function. You meet obligations. You show up. You perform competence. Yet beneath that surface, something essential begins to erode.

What erodes first is not competence, but ambition. The quiet pull toward something better weakens. Curiosity about the future fades into maintenance of the present.

Risk begins to feel unnecessary, even threatening. Patience with difficulty shortens, and effort starts to feel heavier than it should. Life becomes more about managing days than moving toward anything.

Boredom once served a purpose. It created pressure toward action, curiosity, and exploration. It pushed people toward effort, conversation, and risk.

In a hyper-stimulated environment, boredom is treated as a problem to be eliminated instantly. A screen resolves it in seconds.

Over time, boredom stops acting like a signal and starts feeling like something to escape.

Relief replaces direction.

This is where pleasure begins to lose its meaning. Not because pleasure is wrong, but because it arrives without context. Reward detaches from effort.

Desire exists without pursuit. Stimulation becomes something to consume rather than something that follows engagement with life.

The cost of this shift is rarely named, even by the people experiencing it. Low motivation, uneven discipline, emotional numbness, and an enduring sense of discontent that cannot be linked to a single source are some of its manifestations.

Many men experience this as a loss of drive. They feel capable, intelligent, and aware, yet unable to sustain momentum toward anything that requires patience.

The common response is self-blame. Laziness. Weak will. A lack of drive. The more effort feels difficult, the more pressure people place on themselves.

That pressure turns into fatigue. Fatigue increases the urge to escape. Escape brings short relief, followed by shame. Shame shrinks ambition, and with it, the willingness to try again.

This interpretation is incorrect and exacerbates the issue. In an overstimulated system, pushing more frequently has the reverse impact when drive wanes. Pressure increases fatigue. Fatigue increases the need for escape.

Escape reinforces the very patterns that suppress motivation in the first place. The cycle tightens, not because the individual lacks insight, but because insight alone does not alter the underlying conditions.

This book describes that process as dopamine debt.

The term is not meant to dramatize ordinary behavior or reduce complex human experience to chemistry. It is a metaphor that serves a purpose.

Short-term stimulation depletes future energy when it is used frequently to control mood, tension, or boredom. Drive does not disappear, but it becomes harder to access.

Effort feels heavier. Focus feels fragile. Direction becomes difficult to maintain.

Naming this pattern matters. Problems without language feel personal. Problems with language become observable.

The chapters that follow do not rush toward solutions. They begin with recognition. Here, awareness is shown as an orientation rather than a remedy.

Many individuals feel powerless to stop even if they already know what they are doing. That does not indicate weakness. It indicates that the trap operates at a psychological and environmental level, not an intellectual one.

What follows begins with observation rather than correction. It lingers on the patterns that have become normal, the habits that feel automatic, and the quiet confusion that comes from knowing something is wrong without being able to name it.

The aim is not to fix anything yet, but to see clearly what has been shaping attention, desire, and motivation from the inside.

The intention is simply to help you notice what has quietly taken the place of what once felt natural.

The second part stays with the feeling of being stuck, even when understanding is already there. It looks at why effort so often turns into exhaustion, and why slipping back feels less like failure and more like part of the pattern.

Only after that foundation is established does the book turn toward rebuilding. Not through deprivation or intensity, but through design.

Environment over willpower. Structure over force. Small, repeatable changes that restore effort as something that feels meaningful again.

This is not a book about quitting pleasure. Pleasure is not the enemy. Unconscious pleasure is. When stimulation becomes automatic, it stops serving life and starts replacing it.

The mechanisms of overstimulation are shared, even if their effects are expressed differently.

This book focuses on men, where the cost most often appears as muted ambition, emotional withdrawal, and quiet disengagement.

Where relevant, parallel observations will show how these same forces appear in women, without altering the underlying principles.

Over the long term, the cost is rarely dramatic. Years pass without obvious collapse. Ambitions soften rather than shatter. Curiosity narrows. Life becomes smaller by degrees, not through failure, but through quiet repetition. Nothing feels broken enough to demand change, yet something essential is slowly lost.

There are no heroic transformations promised here. Progress in this domain is subtle. A slightly longer attention span. Fewer compulsive checks. Effort that feels marginally more rewarding than before.

These changes rarely announce themselves, but they compound over time.

This book does not offer a perfect ending. It offers a way of seeing that makes autopilot harder to sustain.

Awareness strong enough to interrupt patterns that once felt invisible. Agency that emerges gradually, without drama.

Not to become ascetic.
Not to withdraw from modern life.
But to live it deliberately.

This preface is not an argument. It is an orientation.
What follows is observation before judgment, understanding before action, and rebuilding without violence toward the self.

No promises.
No ultimatums.

Just a clearer view of what has been happening, and what becomes possible once you can no longer pretend you did not notice.

Before continuing, there is nothing you need to change or decide. Simply notice what feels familiar as you read. Notice the moments of recognition, the quiet resistance, and the sense that something described here has been part of your life longer than you realized.

This book does not ask for effort yet. It asks for attention. Not the kind that strains, but the kind that stays. Awareness, when sustained gently, alters what can no longer remain automatic.

That is where this work begins. Not with discipline or denial, but with seeing clearly enough that unconscious patterns start to lose their grip.

Chapter 1 - The First Hit

Aarav remains awake at 11:47 p.m.

His math textbook is spread open on his desk with the spine bent. The pages slightly twisted at the corners from months of usage. The problem at the top of the page waits.

The pencil rests diagonally over a partially completed equation that tails off mid-line like a discarded object in transit.

Next to his hand is the phone, face up.

He tells himself he'll check it once more before finishing the assignment. Just a quick scroll. Five minutes. The kind of break that feels harmless because it has no edges.

His thumb moves without urgency. The screen brightens. A short video begins before he consciously decides to watch it. Someone is speaking fast. Subtitles flash. There is music layered underneath.

The tape stops, and another one starts right away, matched to what he lingered on the last time with eerie accuracy.

The first five minutes go by without his noticing.

He leans back comfortably in his seat in the dark room except for the blue-white illumination. The light silently pulses over his face.

The night outside his window has already grown extremely quiet. Even the mildest sounds are more noticeable. There is a dog barking in the distance.

On the screen, something funny. Then something impressive. Then something slightly provocative. Then something mildly infuriating.

Before fading into the following clip, each one offers a brief burst of sensation, such as surprise, laughter, interest, or annoyance.

"I'm relaxed," he assures himself.

He is not actually at ease. He has a really particular kind of alertness. His thumb is poised while his gaze remains steady. He seems to be waiting for something a little better than what has happened, as seen by the little gap behind his brow and the imperceptible strain in his chest.

It may be the next one.

That feeling—small, electric, almost invisible—is not satisfaction. It is anticipation.

Midnight arrives quietly. Aarav does not register it.

An hour ago, he made a half-line effort on his schoolwork, but it is still incomplete. At one point, he briefly examines the equation as if it were someone else's.

The numbers look heavier than they did earlier. Less inviting. The idea of leaning forward and thinking feels disproportionate to the task itself.

"I'll finish it in the morning," he thinks. "I work better under pressure anyway."

The thought lands smoothly. It feels reasonable. Responsible, even.

Another video loads.

He is not chasing pleasure in any dramatic sense. There is no overwhelming rush, no ecstatic immersion. What he is chasing is subtler than that. He is chasing the next flicker of something slightly more interesting than the last.

The architecture of the feed ensures that he never waits long enough to feel absence. The space between stimulation has been compressed to almost nothing. Silence does not get a turn. Neither does boredom.

He cannot recall the point at which boredom became unbearable to him.

Bored had a different weight when he was younger. It stretched time. It forced him into odd experiments—building things from spare parts, walking outside without a destination, replaying conversations in his head until they turned into imagined futures. It was uncomfortable, but it had edges. It pressed him toward action.

Boredom feels like a bug now.

His hand naturally moves when a space opens up, whether it's standing in line, sitting on the edge of his bed, or taking a break between jobs.
The device fills the space before the discomfort fully forms. There is no deliberate decision involved. The relief arrives preemptively.

He does not consider this unusual. None of his friends do either.

Earlier that evening, a message thread pulsed continuously while he attempted to study. Memes passed through the group like currency. A video clip from a game. A screenshot of someone's comment.

A quick joke, then another. Even silence in the chat felt temporary, as though something was about to happen and he should stay present for it.

Presence, now, means availability.

He flips to another app. Then back again. Then to something else entirely. The transitions are frictionless. There is no sense of leaving one environment and entering another. Everything feels like a continuous stream, a single surface with different textures.

Somewhere beneath the movement is a quiet recalibration taking place.

The brain does not measure pleasure in absolute terms. It measures contrast. It pays attention to change. When a new picture, notion, or signal appears, it triggers a little dopamine surge.

Not as a reward for consuming it, but as a signal that something potentially useful has appeared.

Dopamine, in its simplest sense, is not the chemical of pleasure. It is the chemical of anticipation.

It rises in expectation. It prepares the body to lean forward.

In older environments, anticipation required effort. You waited for a letter to arrive. You practiced a skill before feeling improvement.

You pursued someone before receiving attention. The gap between effort and reward created tension, and that tension carried meaning.

In Aarav's room, the gap has been engineered away.

Each swipe carries the possibility of something slightly better than the last. The cost of finding out is almost zero. No travel. No social risk. No sustained focus. Just a thumb movement measured in millimeters.

His brain adapts quickly.

When rewards arrive without effort, anticipation begins to detach from pursuit. The system that once mobilized energy for action now activates for passive consumption. The spike still occurs, but it no longer leads anywhere beyond the next swipe.

Over time, the baseline shifts.

The more frequently the mind is lifted by small, rapid bursts of novelty, the more ordinary states begin to feel comparatively dull.

Homework, which unfolds slowly and demands concentration before offering satisfaction, cannot compete with a stream of unpredictable novelty delivered in seconds.

This is not a moral failing. It is a calibration process.

Aarav yawns but does not feel sleepy. His body is tired, yet his mind remains lightly stimulated, hovering just above rest. He scrolls past something meaningful without absorbing it. He pauses briefly on something trivial. The algorithm notices both.

He thinks, "Just one more," though he does not specify one more of what.

At 12:26 a.m., he finally places the phone face-down. The sudden darkness in the room feels louder than expected. He lies back on his bed and stares at the ceiling.

The silence presses in.

Without the steady drip of novelty, his thoughts begin to surface in uneven fragments. The unfinished homework. The test next week. The subtle anxiety about falling slightly behind. None of it is catastrophic. All of it is manageable. Yet in the absence of stimulation, it feels heavier.

He reaches for the phone again before fully deciding to do so.

The relief is immediate.

What is happening in this room is not dramatic. There is no visible collapse, no ruined future unfolding in real time. Aarav will wake up tomorrow. He will attend school. He will laugh with friends. He will function.

That is precisely what makes the shift difficult to detect.

The change is not in his capability. It is in his relationship to effort.

When stimulation becomes ambient—constant, low-level, always available—the nervous system recalibrates around it. Attention fragments into shorter intervals. Waiting becomes uncomfortable. Activities that unfold slowly begin to feel disproportionately demanding.

This conditioning often begins in adolescence, when the brain is particularly sensitive to reward signals. During these years, neural pathways are refined according to repeated behavior. What is used frequently becomes efficient. What is neglected becomes harder to access.

If anticipation is repeatedly paired with effortless digital novelty, the system learns to expect reward without sustained investment. The association forms quietly. No one announces it.

By the time Aarav notices that studying feels heavier than it once did, the shift has already been integrated into his baseline.

He might interpret the change personally. "Maybe I'm just not disciplined enough," he could think. Or, "I've always been bad at focusing."

Such explanations feel logical because they locate the issue within character. They ignore the environment that has been shaping his nervous system for years.

The platforms he scrolls through are not neutral containers of content. They are engineered ecosystems built to maximize time spent within them. Variable rewards—unpredictable, intermittent bursts of novelty—hold attention more effectively than consistent ones. The uncertainty keeps the anticipation system engaged.

You do not know what the next swipe will bring. That uncertainty is the hook.

In older reward structures, effort preceded outcome. In this one, outcome precedes effort, and effort is optional.

The mismatch accumulates.

Aarav begins to notice that starting tasks requires more negotiation than it used to. He sits at his desk longer before beginning. He checks his phone "one last time" more often. The distance between intention and action grows slightly wider.

Nothing appears broken enough to demand intervention.

Yet something subtle is being borrowed. Motivation feels muted not because desire has vanished, but because the contrast has changed.

The world outside the screen has not become less meaningful. It has become less intense.

Aarav does not articulate this in chemical terms. He experiences it as a faint restlessness when tasks slow down, as a persistent urge to check something even when nothing urgent exists.

During class the next day, he listens for a few minutes before his focus drifts. His hand slips into his pocket almost reflexively. He does not always remove the phone. Sometimes the touch alone is enough—a reassurance that stimulation is within reach.

Boredom, once a corridor leading somewhere, now feels like a wall.

This shift is not confined to him. It is ambient, woven into the design of modern life. Notifications punctuate conversations. Short-form clips compress narrative into seconds.

Dating apps transform human connection into an interface of swipes. The pattern repeats across platforms: minimal effort, immediate feedback, infinite scroll.

The machine does not demand devotion. It offers convenience.

Over time, convenience reshapes expectation.

Aarav finishes his week. He completes assignments, sometimes late. He meets friends. He plays games. He scrolls at night. There is no dramatic reckoning.

Yet in quiet moments—lying in bed, sitting alone on a bus—he senses a vague dissatisfaction that lacks a clear source. It is not intense enough to alarm him. It is simply present.

He wonders, occasionally, why things that once excited him now require negotiation—like the sketchbook he used to open every evening without thinking, which now stays zipped in his drawer. Why the beginning feels heavier than he imagined. Why rest does not fully restore.

He does not connect these questions to the small, repeated spikes of anticipation that structure his evenings.

The first hit was never a single event. It was not a dramatic introduction. It was the gradual normalization of frictionless reward, delivered during years when his brain was still learning what to value and how to pursue it.

When stimulation becomes constant, anticipation detaches from effort. When anticipation detaches from effort, desire loses direction. The system remains active, but it no longer points clearly toward growth.

This is how the trap operates—not through force, but through ease.

There is no villain in Aarav's room. There is only a device, a feed, and a nervous system doing exactly what it was designed to do in an environment it was not designed for.

He sets his alarm. The phone rests inches from his pillow. As he closes his eyes, a faint impulse surfaces—check once more, just in case something happened.

He resists for a moment, then gives in.

The screen lights up.

Somewhere beneath the surface of that small, ordinary gesture, a pattern strengthens. Not enough to be noticed. Not enough to feel dangerous. Just enough to make tomorrow's effort slightly heavier than today's.

Nothing breaks.

The shift continues.

Chapter 2 - Pleasure Without Purpose

Aarav is nineteen now. The hostel where he resides has a slight detergent and stale scent. Fortunately, he no longer detects these smells. The space feels more constrained in comparison to the brochure. The ceiling is lower than he anticipated. The walls are still covered with posters his roommate hung. He never imagined his college to be like this.

He does not feel tired even at 11:42 p.m.

His laptop remains open facing his bed. More out of habit than purpose, the headphones dangle around his neck. Beside the trackpad, his phone lights up every few minutes. Without truly finishing what he's reading, he takes a quick look at it.

The browser has four tabs open at the top.

One plays music softly in the background. One holds a video paused midway. One is a search results page he has not committed to yet. The last is a social media feed he checks between clicks without realizing he has switched.

The movements are clean and automatic. No obvious urgency, labored breathing, or extreme preoccupation are present. It appears to be idle browsing from the outside.

He is searching for a precise sensation that he cannot quite name. Not intensity exactly, and not novelty for its own sake.

He is looking for the moment when something registers more strongly than what came before.

The first video plays for thirty seconds. He drags the cursor forward slightly, testing the next segment. It does not deliver what he expected. He closes the tab and opens another.

Two years ago, refinement was unnecessary. A single video would have held him. The anticipation would build steadily, and the outcome would feel sufficient.

He scrolls longer before selecting. He reads titles more carefully. He compares many windows that are open simultaneously. He begins one and leaves it unfinished, certain something better is just one click away.

That evening, his roommate threw a hoodie at him and asked, "Stepping out tonight?"

"Maybe later," Aarav said, his attention still on the screen. "I need to finish a few things."

His roommate looked over at the laptop. "A few things, huh?"

Aarav smirked without looking up. "Shut up."

There was no judgment in the exchange. Only recognition.

"Bro, I swear," his roommate continued, flopping onto his own bed, "I spend more time looking for something to watch than actually watching it."

"Same," Aarav replied. "Half the time I'm just scrolling."

"Yeah, like nothing's good enough."

A brief silence settled between them.

Then the roommate shrugged. "There's too much content. We're spoiled."

"Yeah," Aarav said again.

The kinds of videos he clicks now are more specific than before. The searches are narrower. The patience is thinner. What once felt immediate now requires filtering.

He types a word into the search bar and watches the results appear: college

The thumbnails populate quickly. Parties, dorm rooms, shaky camera angles. Too broad.

He adds another word and runs the search again: college pov

Closer, but still not quite what he had in mind.

He adjusts the phrase once more, adding another word before pressing enter again: amateur college pov

The results shift again. Different thumbnails this time. He scans them more slowly.

The results shift slightly.

He scrolls halfway down the page, hesitates, then edits the phrase once more before running it again.

Five tabs open in quick succession. He scans the thumbnails without fully registering faces. One looks promising. He lets it play briefly, then skips ahead along the timeline.

The part he expected never arrives.

He closes it.

Back to the search bar.

He adjusts the search phrase and runs it again. Scrolls longer this time. Opens three more. Leaves them buffering in the background while he samples another. The switching is faster now. The evaluation is sharper. Each selection carries a flicker of anticipation that drops almost immediately.

None of it is wrong. None of it is extreme. It simply fails to hold.

He does not consciously think, I need something stronger. Instead, he thinks, This isn't it.

He opens another tab. Watches for a minute. Feels the familiar rise of anticipation. Then the drop comes faster than expected, like a wave that collapses before reaching shore.

He switches again.

Another tab loads. He does not bother reading the title this time. He skips forward instinctively, testing for intensity, for immediacy. For something that holds.

For a moment, it does. Then it passes.

He remains still after the screen stops moving. The music in the background continues for a few seconds before he notices and pauses it. The room feels quieter than it did a minute ago.

He closes one tab. Then another. The browser shrinks back to a blank search bar. For a brief second, the screen reflects his face instead of someone else's.

He clears history without thinking about it. The action is automatic. Efficient. When the laptop lid remains open but idle, the space feels strangely flat.

Rarely does tolerance make an announcement.

When the same stimulus triggers dopamine repeatedly, the brain adjusts. It reduces the sensitivity of its receptors so the signal does not overwhelm the system. This is not punishment. It is regulation. The nervous system is designed to maintain balance, so what once felt intense slowly begins to register as ordinary.

As the threshold shifts, the same input produces a smaller response. Content that once captured attention easily begins to feel insufficient. Not because the person is becoming deviant, but because the brain now requires stronger signals to generate the same level of stimulation. Novelty, intensity, and variation begin to matter more.

Aarav does not think in terms of receptors or thresholds. He experiences it as restlessness. As the quiet sense that nothing quite lands. As the feeling that something better must exist one click away. The dissatisfaction appears personal, even though the mechanism behind it is predictable.

He remains still after the screen stops moving.

The music in the background continues for a few seconds before he notices and pauses it.

His body registers a faint heaviness that doesn't match how little he has moved. His chest feels slightly hollow. He closes one tab. Then another. The browser shrinks back to a blank search bar.

For a brief second, the dark screen reflects his face. He glances at it and looks away almost immediately. He clears the browsing history without thinking. The action is automatic.

When the laptop sits open but idle, the room feels strangely flat.

He lingers on the blank screen longer than necessary. In time, the searching becomes more interesting than whatever he's looking for.

This is why he sometimes spends twenty minutes searching and five minutes watching. The hunt carries more charge than the capture.

He would not phrase it that way. He would say he is being selective.

But selectivity has quietly turned into restlessness.

He takes a seat to accomplish something. However, he stares at the screen for a long time. The cursor waits for an input by blinking continually. For some reason, he is reluctant to begin.

"I will just quickly check something," he murmurs.

He isn't aware he hasn't begun for ten minutes.

At the gym, he finds himself checking his phone between sets more often than before. The rest periods stretch. The impulse to leave early appears sooner.

Even conversations occasionally lose their grip. There is a hint of frustration when a buddy talks for a long time. His attention is used to quicker shifts, not because he doesn't care.

He keeps this observation to himself.

"Do you ever feel like stuff just doesn't hit the same?" he asks his roommate in a low voice one afternoon as they sit in the school café.

His roommate looks up from his phone. “Like what?”

“I don’t know. Just regular things. Classes. Even going out. It’s fun, but it’s not… I don’t know.”

“Not what?”

“Not enough.”

The roommate laughs lightly. “Man, that’s just dopamine fried brain. We’re cooked.”

“Yeah,” Aarav says.

Late one night, after closing everything, Aarav remains seated in the dim light of his desk lamp.

His phone lies beside him, silent for once. The room is not uncomfortable, but it is unadorned by noise.

He tries to recall the last time something absorbed him fully without the urge to switch away. A project, perhaps. A conversation that extended without distraction. A goal that pulled him forward instead of needing to be pushed.

The memories surface slowly.

He realizes that pleasure has not disappeared from his life. It has multiplied.

Yet the multiplication has thinned it. He tells himself this phase is temporary.

College is supposed to feel scattered. Everyone says so. Late nights, irregular sleep, inconsistent discipline. It is part of the atmosphere.

But what unsettles him is not the behavior itself. It is how normal it feels.

He spends more time curating stimulation than participating in anything that unfolds slowly. One night, after closing everything, Aarav lies back on his bed staring at the ceiling.

His body feels tired. His mind does not. The laptop sits closed on his desk. He tells himself he's done for the night. He needs sleep.

A faint restlessness builds after a few minutes of stillness. Not urgent. Just enough to make lying there uncomfortable.

He reaches for his phone. Scrolls briefly. Nothing holds.

"Just checking something," he murmurs to no one.

He sits up and opens the laptop. The browser loads.

The search bar blinks.

He types, deletes, and tries another phrase. Scrolls. Then scrolls again.

Within a minute the pattern has returned.

His thumb travels inches. His body remains still. His mind remains semi-engaged but never fully absorbed.

Afterward, he closes the laptop and lies back on his bed. His body feels slightly drained, though he has expended almost no physical energy.

The next morning, his alarm rings.

He hits snooze once. Then again. He feels unusually heavy, though he slept a reasonable number of hours.

There is no sharp guilt. Just reluctance.

He stares at the ceiling and negotiates with himself.

"I'll start being more disciplined next week," he thinks. "This week's already messy."

The thought feels rational. Strategic, even.

He does not connect the heaviness to the repeated cycles of high-intensity stimulation followed by abrupt drops. He experiences it as fatigue.

By midday, he feels normal again.

By night, the cycle resumes.

Over weeks, something subtle shifts in his ambition.

He still talks about plans and internships when the topic comes up.

But the emotional charge behind those plans feels weaker than it once did.

When boredom surfaces, it no longer pushes him toward reflection or experimentation. It pushes him toward consumption.

The corridor that once led somewhere now loops back to the screen.

During a study session at the library, he catches himself switching tabs repeatedly while attempting to research.

The assignment prompt sits at the top of the screen. A simple literature review. Three sources. Two pages. Something he could normally finish in an hour.

He opens the first article and begins reading. The paragraphs are clear, the argument straightforward. Halfway through the second section, his attention loosens.

A notification appears in the corner of the screen. He clicks it without thinking. One tab becomes three. Then five.

A news headline. A short video. A quick glance at social media.

He returns to the article, scrolls back to the paragraph he left, and tries again.

Two minutes later another tab opens.

A friend sitting across from him whispers, "You locked in?"

"Yeah," Aarav replies automatically.

He finishes the assignment eventually, but it takes longer than necessary. The work feels heavier than its difficulty warrants.

Walking back to the dorm, he feels a faint irritation toward himself.

"I used to focus better," he thinks.

The statement lingers.

Aarav begins to notice impatience creeping into conversations. When a story unfolds slowly, his mind searches for acceleration. When a professor explains a concept step by step, he feels the urge to compress it.

He is not rude. He does not interrupt.

He simply disengages internally.

One weekend, he attends a small gathering at a friend's apartment. Music plays softly in the background. People sit in loose circles talking.

Someone across the room is explaining a story about an internship interview gone wrong. The group laughs at the right moments. Aarav nods along, half-listening.

His phone lights up in his hand.

A notification. Nothing important. He glances at it anyway.

A short video begins to play without sound. Thirty seconds. Then another. He scrolls once, then again. Voices continue around him. Someone asks a question he doesn't fully hear.

He looks up and nods as if he's been following the conversation. For a moment he tries to stay present. He locks the screen and places the phone on the table.

The conversation stretches slowly. Someone begins telling a longer story. His attention loosens again. A minute later the phone is back in his hand.

"Bro, you're here, right?"

"Yeah," Aarav says quickly, locking his screen. "I'm listening."

But he realizes he is not fully there. The room feels under-stimulating compared to the density he has grown accustomed to.

Later that night, walking back alone, he feels an unexpected hollowness.

This is the quiet danger of pleasure without purpose.

When reward detaches from effort, and effort detaches from meaning, life does not collapse. It thins.

But the internal sense of momentum weakens.

Ambition softens to match energy.

One night, after another cycle of searching and closing and reopening, he sits still longer than usual.

The laptop screen reflects faintly in his darkened window. His own face looks back at him, slightly distorted.

He feels neither shame nor satisfaction.

He feels neutral.

That neutrality unsettles him more than guilt would have.

Guilt at least signals conflict. Neutrality signals normalization.

He closes the laptop and remains seated in silence.

There was a time when desire pulled him toward things. Projects. Ideas. Skills he wanted to build. Conversations he wanted to initiate.

Now desire pulls him toward relief. Relief is immediate. Direction is distant.

He sets the phone down beside him. The room feels unusually still. Nothing has broken in his life. But something has drifted.

And drift, left unattended, rarely announces how far it has carried you until the shore you once recognized is no longer visible.

Chapter 3 – The Dopamine Debt

The alarm goes off at 6:30 a.m.

Aarav opens his eyes slowly. The sound appears distant, repetitive, a little irritating, and not urgent enough to force movement through the veil of slumber.

His phone rattles on the nightstand's wooden top. He remains still for a short while, awaiting the second tremor.

When it comes, his hand moves automatically across the mattress until his fingers find the edge of the device. The screen lights his face before he is fully awake.

6:30. He taps snooze. The room falls quiet again.

Outside the window the city has already begun moving. A truck downshifts somewhere in the distance. Someone's footsteps pass along the sidewalk below. Morning sounds, steady and indifferent.

Aarav closes his eyes again.

The heaviness in his body does not feel like ordinary tiredness. It feels closer to gravity. As though the mattress has gained weight overnight and his muscles must negotiate with it before standing.

Nine minutes later the alarm returns.

He opens his eyes halfway this time. Once more, the screen illuminates the dimly lit space with a light blue hue.

At 6:39, he hits sleep once again. For a moment he remains on the lock screen.

A notification banner slides quietly across the display. Then another. Messages. A news alert. Something from an app he does not remember installing.

His thumb moves before he fully decides to unlock the phone. The night before appears in fragments.

The screen unlocked to the familiar grid of icons. Without thinking, Aarav tapped the red YouTube icon. The app opened directly to a short video already playing.

A man stood in front of a whiteboard explaining why a particular tech stock was about to crash. Lines and arrows covered the board. Aarav watched for maybe forty seconds before the man began repeating the same point, and his thumb flicked upward.

The next video loaded instantly. A gym transformation montage—before and after photos sliding across the screen while loud motivational music played. He watched the whole thing, thirty-eight seconds, then the feed moved on.

Another video appeared. A comedian doing a quick sketch about office meetings that could have been emails. Aarav smirked once, then scrolled before the punchline finished.

A notification banner slid down from the top of the screen. His college group chat had become active again.

He switched to WhatsApp.

Three new messages waited. A meme about Monday mornings. Someone replying with laughing emojis. Then a video link.

He tapped it.

A basketball highlight opened. A slow-motion dunk from a player he didn't recognize. The crowd roared through the phone speaker before he muted it and switched back to the feed.

YouTube loaded another short automatically. A woman describing her "5 a.m. morning routine." Coffee. Journaling. A perfectly organized desk. Aarav watched quietly for almost a minute before the pacing slowed and he flicked his thumb again.

A news clip appeared next. Two commentators arguing about politics. Aarav watched the first twenty seconds, then skipped.

Next came a cooking video. Pasta tossed through a pan with garlic and olive oil. It actually looked good. For a moment he imagined making it someday, then the thought disappeared as he scrolled again.

Another notification appeared. He glanced at the time in the corner of the screen.

11:47.

That seemed later than expected, but not late enough to matter.

The next few videos blurred together. A travel clip showing cliffs somewhere in Greece. A productivity tip about waking up earlier. A quick clip of a dog running across a frozen lake.

Each held his attention just long enough before the next one replaced it.

At some point he switched apps without really deciding to. Instagram opened to a reel of someone reviewing inexpensive tech gadgets.

He watched a small desk lamp turn on and off three different colors. The reviewer said it cost twelve dollars. Aarav kept watching until the end, then scrolled again.

A fitness influencer appeared explaining the "three biggest mistakes people make at the gym." Aarav listened to the first one before his thumb moved automatically.

More reels loaded.

A travel vlogger standing on a crowded street in Tokyo. A quick recipe for protein pancakes. A clip from a podcast where two men debated whether motivation was overrated.

Aarav watched that one longer than most.

Eventually the pace of scrolling slowed for a moment. The room around him had grown completely quiet.

He checked the time again.

12:23.

He shifted slightly on the pillow and told himself the same thing he had told himself dozens of nights before.

One more video.

The next clip was a street interview. Someone asking strangers how much money they had saved by age thirty. Aarav watched until a man answered "around two hundred thousand," then scrolled immediately.

Another video. A cinematic drone shot of mountains somewhere in Norway.

Another. A clip of a stand-up comedian telling a story about airport security.

Another.

Time moved without much resistance.

At some point his phone slipped slightly in his hand and the brightness of the screen caught his attention again. He glanced at the clock in the corner.

1:14.

That number felt different. Late enough to notice.

He hesitated for a moment, then nodded slightly to himself.

Okay. Last one.

The next video began automatically. A creator explaining a simple productivity system using colored sticky notes. Aarav watched the first half with mild interest before another video replaced it.

Then another.

By the time he finally locked the screen and set the phone beside him, the room had already gone silent again.

He cannot remember the exact moment he decided to sleep. The alarm vibrates again.

6:48.

Aarav exhales slowly and rolls onto his back. The ceiling above him appears slightly blurred while his eyes adjust.

He slept more than six hours. Enough, technically. However, the thought of sitting up seems oddly out of scale to the actual movement.

His thoughts start negotiating in silence. Five more minutes. Just enough to wake up properly.

He sets the phone down beside him but does not close his eyes. Instead he watches the screen darken as the display times out.

The room returns to its dim morning gray. A faint restlessness appears almost immediately. Not urgency. Just the sense that something is missing.

His hand reaches for the phone again.

The screen lights instantly in his hand.

Three notifications wait on the lock screen. A text from his mother asking if he is awake yet. A news alert about a market drop. A promotion from a shopping app announcing a flash sale that ends today.

His thumb ignores the messages and taps a video notification instead.

A short clip begins automatically. A man speaking quickly about a simple productivity trick—something about organizing tasks using color-coded notes. Subtitles flash across the screen as the man talks.

Aarav watches for maybe twenty seconds before scrolling.

Another video replaces it immediately. A sports highlight—someone hitting a deep three-point shot while the crowd erupts. He watches until the replay begins, then flicks upward again.

He is still lying flat on his back. The phone hovers a few inches above his face while the pale blue light fills the gray morning room.

The next clip loads.

A woman explaining how she prepares her morning coffee routine. Beans grinding. Steam rising from a metal kettle. Aarav watches quietly until the pacing slows.

His thumb moves again.

A cooking video appears. Someone slicing garlic and tossing it into a hot pan. Oil crackles loudly through the tiny speaker before he scrolls past it.

The feed refreshes.

A travel clip now. A drone camera flying across a coastline somewhere bright and unfamiliar. The water looks impossibly blue.

Aarav watches for a moment longer than the others.

Then he scrolls again.

The movement has become automatic now. Watch. Flick. Watch. Flick.

His body remains heavy against the mattress, but his attention sharpens slightly as the images change.

Somewhere outside a truck shifts gears on the street.

Aarav briefly glances at the clock in the corner of the screen.

6:48.

That seems early enough not to matter.

Another video loads. Then another.

At some point the sound of the room returns—the faint hum of the city waking outside the window.

Then the phone vibrates suddenly in his hand. The alarm.

7:03.

Aarav blinks at the screen, surprised. Fifteen minutes had passed without him noticing. He tells himself he is simply waking up.

After all, no one expects clarity in the first minutes of the morning. Another video loads. Then another. The screen keeps moving, but the room around him stays still.

The noise of the metropolis increases outside. Once more, the alarm vibrates.

7:03.

Aarav blinks at the screen. He had meant to stand up before this one. He taps snooze again.

For a brief moment he considers placing the phone back on the nightstand and getting up immediately.

Instead, he watches one more clip.

Then another.

The action is heavier than anticipated when he eventually sits up straight.

He swings his feet to the floor, his shoulders sagging a little.

Nothing about the morning is catastrophic.

There is no panic. No sense of failure.

He will shower. He will leave the apartment. He will arrive at work only slightly later than he planned.

Yet beneath the routine, something feels subtly misaligned.

The effort required to begin the day seems larger than the day itself.

While the coffee machine hums in the kitchen, Aarav leans against the counter scrolling through messages he has already read once.

The warm bitterness of the first sip registers faintly.

He checks the time again.

7:21.

His laptop bag rests by the door exactly where he left it the night before.

The gym shoes he intended to wear this morning sit beside the door, exactly where he placed them the night before.

Aarav pauses in the kitchen doorway and looks at them. The coffee machine hums softly behind him.

The thought arrives quietly.

He should go.

Not a full workout. Nothing ambitious. Just thirty minutes at the gym downstairs. Enough to start the day properly.

For a moment he imagines it.

Changing into gym clothes. Walking out the door. The familiar smell of rubber mats and metal weights. The first few minutes on the treadmill while the body slowly wakes up.

It would feel better than this heaviness.

He takes another sip of coffee and keeps looking at the shoes. Then his body answers before the decision fully forms.

The idea of changing clothes feels strangely exhausting. Finding the gym shirt. Tying the laces. Walking downstairs.

The effort expands in his mind. A counter-thought appears almost immediately. Tomorrow will be better.

Today he is already slightly late. The morning started slowly. A rushed workout would only make the rest of the day feel scattered.

Tomorrow he could do it properly.

Wake up earlier. Six o'clock instead of six thirty. Get real sleep tonight.

He could start the routine cleanly from the beginning. The logic assembles itself easily.

Tomorrow he will have more energy. More time. The workout would actually count.

Today would just be forcing it. Aarav takes another sip of coffee while the thought settles.

The shoes remain by the door. For a brief moment he almost reaches for them anyway. Then the reasoning closes the argument. Tomorrow.

The decision lands softly, without resistance. A small sense of relief follows. He places the mug in the sink and reaches for his phone.

He places the empty mug in the sink and reaches for his phone again while putting on his jacket. The gesture feels natural. Automatic. Nothing in Aarav's life appears broken.

His job functions. His relationships remain intact. His plans for the future still exist in conversation when someone asks.

Yet mornings like this have become common. The alarm rings. He wakes up. And the simple act of beginning the day feels slightly heavier than it should.

Many people experience this shift without questioning it. They assume the problem is discipline.

Perhaps they stayed up too late. Perhaps they lack motivation. Perhaps they simply need to push harder tomorrow.

But motivation rarely disappears without a reason. More often, it has been quietly spent somewhere else. What Aarav feels this morning is not unusual fatigue.

It is the subtle aftereffect of a nervous system that has already consumed much of its stimulation before the day even begins.

The night offered dozens of small rewards—each one brief, each one easy to access.

None of them felt significant in isolation.

Together, they produced a steady stream of anticipation.

Each swipe carried the possibility that the next moment might be slightly more interesting than the last.

The brain responds strongly to that possibility.

Dopamine does not rise primarily from pleasure itself. It rises in anticipation. The signal prepares the body for pursuit.

In environments where effort once preceded reward, that anticipation pushed people toward action. Toward solving problems. Toward building something that did not yet exist.

But modern streams of stimulation trigger the same signal without requiring pursuit.

A swipe is enough.

The anticipation still appears. The nervous system still prepares for engagement. Yet the engagement rarely extends beyond the next piece of content.

Over time the brain adjusts to this pattern.

Not as punishment, but as calibration.

When stimulation arrives frequently and without effort, the nervous system lowers its baseline sensitivity. The spikes remain, but the ordinary moments between them begin to feel flatter.

Tasks that unfold slowly—writing an email, preparing for work, exercising—must now compete with memories of far denser stimulation.

They are not less meaningful.

They are simply less intense.

And intensity is what the system has learned to expect.

Aarav does not experience this process as neurochemistry. He experiences it as reluctance. As the quiet sense that beginning something requires more energy than it once did.

This is what can be described as dopamine debt.

Short bursts of easy stimulation borrow motivation from the future. The night feels engaging. But the cost appears later as inertia.

By morning, the drive that normally supports effort has already been partially spent.

What looks like laziness is often motivation already used elsewhere.

People rarely recognize this connection. Instead they interpret the experience personally. They assume something inside them has weakened.

That they have lost discipline. That their ambition has quietly faded. So they respond the only way they know how. They apply pressure. Wake earlier. Push harder. Force concentration through willpower.

Sometimes this works briefly. More often it produces fatigue. Fatigue invites escape. Escape arrives in the same form it did the night before: frictionless stimulation.

The relief feels harmless. Yet the cycle quietly continues. Stimulation releases anticipation. Anticipation spends motivation.

Low motivation increases the urge to escape. Escape returns to stimulation.

Aarav finishes dressing and checks the time again before leaving his apartment.

7:38.

He is running slightly later than planned, but the difference is small enough not to matter.

Outside, the morning air feels cooler than expected.

As he walks toward the subway entrance, Aarav's phone vibrates in his pocket.

He pulls it out without thinking. A notification from Instagram. Someone he follows has posted a new reel.

He opens it while walking.

A video begins playing. A man explaining why certain everyday foods are "secretly damaging your metabolism." Aarav watches for a few seconds while descending the stairs toward the platform.

The video slows near the middle. His thumb flicks upward.

Another clip loads. A travel video—drone footage sweeping across a coastline somewhere bright and distant. The train platform comes into view ahead of him.

A message notification appears at the top of the screen.

A friend has sent a link. Aarav opens it briefly, reads the headline, then returns to the video feed without replying.

He steps onto the platform and moves closer to the yellow line.

Across the tracks, a woman in her forties sits on a bench reading a paperback book. Her phone rests inside her bag.

For a moment Aarav notices the stillness of it.

Then his phone vibrates again.

Another video loads automatically. Someone explaining a simple productivity system using a whiteboard and colored markers. Aarav watches without sound.

A rush of wind pushes through the station.

The train arrives.

Aarav looks up just in time as the doors slide open. He steps inside while the video continues playing in his hand.

He finds a seat near the door.

By the time the train begins moving, the video has already changed again.

Nothing dramatic has happened in Aarav's life. He will arrive at work. He will complete the tasks expected of him. He will speak with colleagues and respond to emails.

From the outside, the day will appear normal. Yet beneath the routine, the quiet cost of yesterday's stimulation has already been paid.

Effort today feels slightly heavier than it otherwise would have.

Focus will require more negotiation. Momentum will arrive more slowly. This is how dopamine debt accumulates. Not through collapse.

Through small withdrawals from tomorrow's motivation, repeated so often that the cost begins to feel normal. Nothing breaks. The system continues functioning.

And the difference, though subtle, compounds over time.

Chapter 4 — Reels, Swipes, and Synthetic Validation

At 10:18 p.m., Aarav refreshes Tinder.

The motion is small. The usual stack of faces reappears as if nothing had happened in the world beyond his screen, followed by a quick white flash and a downward tug of his thumb.

Nothing occurs for a second. Next, a notice appears close to the top. It's a contest.

A subtle warmth permeates his chest. Not excitement exactly. More like a brief upward correction, as if something inside him had been gently lifted into alignment.

He opens the chat immediately. No message yet. Just her name, her photos, the blinking cursor in the empty text field waiting for initiative.

He studies her pictures more carefully now than he did while swiping. A mirror selfie. A beach photo. A close-up where she isn't quite smiling but isn't serious either.

He tries to infer a personality from fragments. After a few seconds, he types "Hey." Then deletes it. Types "Hi." Deletes that too.

The cursor blinks, unconcerned and patient.

He sets the phone on the couch next him and locks it, as if being far away may make the situation seem less vulnerable. With the exception of the refrigerator's soft hum, the room is once again quiet.

He checks at his phone once again after thirty seconds. Nothing yet.

Although the sport goes on, the emotional rush has already started to wane. This gave way to a little tightness in his chest that seems eerily like aimless expectancy.

It does not matter, he assures himself. There are more profiles. There are always more profiles. He returns to the main screen and begins swiping again.

Left. Left. Left. Right. Left.

Each motion takes less than a second. A decision without deliberation, guided more by pattern recognition than thought.

Faces blur into categories. Attractive. Not attractive. Uncertain. Not worth the time to evaluate further.

A woman laughing in a group photo. Another posing with a dog. Another standing on a mountain overlook, arms spread toward a horizon he does not recognize.

The app does not present people as people. It presents them as options. Compressed identities optimized for rapid judgment, stripped of context and consequence.

Another right swipe. No match. Then another. Nothing.

Aarav does not feel rejected. There is no moment where someone actively declines him. The absence registers more like silence than refusal.

Rejection without friction is harder to process.

Swiping eventually develops a rhythmic, almost calming quality. The seamless animation of one face replacing another, the slight sound the program produces with each action, and the appearance of forward motion.

It feels like progress without direction.

A Netflix series is neglected on the television across the room. He doesn't notice the artificial laughter that punctuates the rising and falling dialogue.

The smaller, brighter rectangle in his grasp captures all of his attention. Another right swipe. It's a match.

His posture shifts subtly. His shoulders straighten. Proof of desirability, delivered instantly. He opens the profile.

She is smiling in most of her photos. Outdoors in nearly all of them. Wet hair placed behind her ears when hiking, kayaking, or standing next to a waterfall.

Though the picture seems flimsy and more like an idea of a meeting than a scenario, he imagines what it may be like to meet her.

The blank text area awaits once more.

He types, “Hey, how’s your week going?” Reads it. Deletes “how’s.” Types it again. Adds a smiley face. Removes the smiley face.

He sends it before he can reconsider. The message appears on the screen, suddenly permanent. Now the waiting begins.

Aarav places the phone face-down on his thigh, then flips it back over almost immediately. The status beneath her name still reads “Matched today.”

He returns to swiping.

Left. Left. Right. Left. The faces continue.

A woman with professionally lit photos that feel almost corporate in their polish. Another with blurry images taken in dim bars. Another whose entire profile consists of group pictures, forcing him to guess which person she is.

He swipes left on uncertainty. The app rewards decisiveness.

He pauses on one profile longer than usual.

She is not dramatically beautiful, but there is something grounded about her expression. A softness around the eyes. A photo of her reading on a couch instead of posing somewhere impressive.

He hesitates. Then swipes right. No match.

A faint disappointment registers, sharper than the others because it followed hesitation. He scrolls back instinctively, as if the decision could be undone.

It cannot. The profile is gone. He continues.

After fifteen minutes, his thumb begins to move without conscious input. The decisions blur together. Attraction becomes less about genuine interest and more about maintaining the rhythm.

Aarav leans back into the couch. A notification appears at the top of the screen. The first match has replied.

His heart rate ticks upward before he even reads the message.

"Hey :)"

Relief arrives first, then a quick spike of anticipation. Conversation is possible again. The connection, however minimal, has been activated.

He responds immediately.

"Hi. How's your night going?"

She replies within a minute. Short answers. Polite. Noncommittal.

The exchange continues for several messages, each one slightly thinner than the last, like a thread stretched too far. No clear direction, no shared momentum.

Eventually her responses slow.

Then stop.

No goodbye. No conclusion. Just silence suspended at the end of the chat like an unfinished sentence.

Aarav stares at the screen longer than necessary. As if the interaction simply lost altitude and disappeared from radar. He returns to the swipe screen.

The match still exists. The conversation thread remains visible. Proof that something happened, even if it led nowhere.

Another profile appears.

This one is striking. Professionally shot photos, confident posture, a caption that reads more like a brand statement than a biography.

He swipes right without hesitation.

It's a match.

The match lands harder this time — less hope, more scoreboard. He does not message her immediately. Instead, he closes the app and opens Instagram.

Her profile appears at the top of his suggestions almost instantly, as if the platforms are communicating behind the scenes. Thousands of followers. Carefully curated images. Comments filled with fire emojis and short declarations of admiration.

He scrolls through her photos, comparing himself invisibly to the men who have already expressed interest.

The match begins to feel less like connection and more like proximity to status.

He returns to Tinder.

Still no message from her.

The initial surge fades, replaced by a quieter, more ambiguous sensation. Pride mixed with doubt. Validation diluted by uncertainty.

Did she swipe right thoughtfully, or casually? Is he one of many? Will she ever respond at all?

Back in Aarav's apartment, the television episode ends and a new one begins. He has not moved.

He refreshes Tinder again.

No new matches.

The absence feels louder now because it follows expectation.

He switches to Instagram Reels, seeking a different kind of stimulation. Short videos cascade down the screen—travel clips, fitness advice, comedic sketches, strangers living compressed highlight versions of their lives.

Each one produces a tiny flicker of engagement, none of them lasting. Pure consumption, clean and predictable.

After several minutes, he returns to Tinder as if checking a slot machine that might have paid out while he was away.

Still nothing. He sets the phone down and leans his head back against the couch.

He opens the app again. Swipe. Swipe. Swipe. A match appears.

He messages her. She responds. The conversation flows slightly better this time, touching briefly on work, favorite restaurants, the city they both inhabit but experience separately.

For a moment, it almost feels like connection.

Then she stops replying.

He waits a few minutes. Sends another message, lighter this time, an attempt to revive the momentum without appearing needy.

No response.

The chat freezes in place.

Aarav exhales slowly through his nose, a reaction so subtle he barely notices it. Not anger. Not sadness. Something closer to depletion.

He closes the conversation.

The match remains, preserved like an artifact of a moment that never fully materialized.

Matches deliver a form of validation that requires almost nothing from either person. No vulnerability, no sustained attention, no risk of real rejection.

A mutual swipe confirms only that two strangers found each other acceptable for a fraction of a second. It says nothing about compatibility, curiosity, or intention.

Because the signal is so easy to produce, quantity begins to replace meaning. The number of matches becomes a metric of worth, even though it measures reach rather than resonance.

One match feels encouraging; ten should feel decisive. Yet each additional one carries less emotional weight than the last, flattening into statistics rather than experiences.

When conversation demands effort — attention, timing, personality — the return becomes uncertain again. Replies may slow, interest may fade, silence may follow.

Swiping, by contrast, offers immediate feedback with minimal exposure. So the cycle resets: match, brief engagement, diminishing payoff, return to the feed.

Over time, the baseline for what counts as validation quietly rises, while genuine connection becomes harder to recognize when it appears.

The same dynamics operate across the app for women, though the signals arrive differently. Instead of scarcity, there is often volume — messages, likes, profile views accumulating faster than they can be meaningfully processed.

Visibility becomes its own feedback loop, a steady stream of proof that one is being noticed without clarifying who, if anyone, is truly interested.

Conversations begin easily but dissipate just as quickly, buried under newer notifications or fading into silence without resolution. The uncertainty remains intact: attention does not guarantee intention.

In this environment, being seen becomes routine while being known remains rare, and the abundance of options produces its own form of distance.

By midnight, he has accumulated several matches, a handful of short exchanges, and no plans.

Subjectively, it feels like drinking saltwater.

Each sip promises relief and delivers thirst.

Dating apps run on a pattern psychologists call variable rewards — outcomes delivered unpredictably enough to keep anticipation alive. Most swipes lead nowhere. Occasionally one produces a match.

Rarely, a conversation. The brain learns that the next action might resolve the uncertainty, so it continues, not for what it receives, but for the possibility of receiving something.

The design is not accidental. Intermittent reinforcement sustains engagement far longer than consistent results. If every swipe matched, the novelty would collapse.

If none did, the effort would stop. The irregularity keeps the system open, like a slot machine that pays out just often enough to remain believable.

For Aarav, each refresh carries the faint promise that something different could appear — someone interesting, responsive, meaningful.

Most of the time it does not. But the cost of checking is low, and the potential payoff feels personal. The uncertainty itself becomes the stimulus.

He stands and walks to the kitchen, phone still in hand. The apartment is clean, orderly, unmistakably lived in by one person.

A single plate in the drying rack. One coffee mug.

He opens the refrigerator without looking away from the screen, scanning for something to eat while swiping with his other hand.

Nothing appeals.

He closes the door and returns to the couch.

Another match. Another empty chat box.

He continues not because it feels good, but because stopping would leave him alone with the silence the app had been masking.

Eventually he sets the phone down on the coffee table.

The room expands around him immediately, larger and quieter than it seemed before. Without the steady drip of faces and notifications, his thoughts begin to surface.

Across the room, the television continues playing to no one. He picks up the phone again. Not out of desire. Out of habit.

Tinder opens to the same stack of faces, refreshed but fundamentally unchanged. New people, identical experience.

Swipe. Left. Right. No match.

He feels neither hopeful nor discouraged. Just engaged enough to continue. He tells himself he will stop after the next match. Then after the next one. Then after one more.

At 12:47 a.m., he finally closes the app.

The silence that follows is not peaceful. It is hollow, like a room after furniture has been removed.

He sits there for a while, hands resting loosely in his lap, unsure what to do with them now that they are no longer occupied.

Connection was the goal. Validation was the product. Neither has filled the space.

Somewhere in the distance, a car passes on the street below, its tires whispering against the asphalt. The sound fades quickly, leaving the apartment exactly as it was before.

Aarav looks at his phone one last time. No new notifications. He turns off the screen.

In the darkness, the faint afterimage of the interface lingers in his vision, a ghost of faces and icons burned temporarily into his eyes.

For a brief moment, he considers deleting the app.

Not dramatically. Not as a grand gesture. Just as an experiment in quiet.

Instead, he sets the phone on the table within easy reach.

Tomorrow, he tells himself, he will use it more deliberately.

Tomorrow he will message with intention. Ask better questions. Suggest meeting sooner. Treat people like people instead of profiles.

The plan feels reasonable in the dark.

Morning will dilute it.

He leans back against the couch and closes his eyes. The apartment hums softly around him, indifferent to whether he is alone by circumstance or by design.

Somewhere inside him, a quiet recognition forms, difficult to articulate but impossible to ignore. Being seen is not the same as being known.

And being chosen, repeatedly and briefly, is not the same as being kept. The phone remains within arm's reach. He does not pick it up again. But he does not move it away either.

The app will repopulate. And the next small surge of synthetic validation will feel, for a moment, like hope.

Chapter 5 — Desire, Direction, and Energy

Understanding Drive Without Mythology

At 6:12 p.m., Aarav strengthens his hold on a barbell that hasn't yet shown any discernible resistance.

The gym is in its typical post-office bustle. nor calm, nor crowded. From above, flat white lights dazzle. Every action is reflected back into the room by wall-length mirrors, creating an atmosphere of restless activity.

Just loud enough to fill the emptiness without overwhelming the mind, music surges overhead.

Aarav unravels the bar and sinks into a squat.

Down. Pause. Up.

The movement is controlled, technically sound. His knees track properly. His back remains straight. He has done this often enough that the mechanics require little conscious attention.

He racks the bar and exhales. Not exhaustion. Not relief. Just completion.

He steps back and reaches for his phone, already resting on the floor beside his water bottle. The screen lights instantly in his hand. Notifications bloom across the display.

A message from a coworker. A promotional email. A news alert. Two unread messages in a group chat he muted months ago.

His thumb moves through them without reading closely. None require immediate response. None hold him.

He opens Instagram instead.

A short video begins automatically. Someone demonstrating a "three-step morning routine for unstoppable productivity." He watches long enough to register the structure, then scrolls before the explanation finishes.

Another video replaces it. A bodybuilder posing under dramatic lighting, muscles sharply defined, captions listing training tips in rapid succession. Aarav watches longer this time, comparing the physique automatically to his own reflection in the mirror behind the screen.

Then he scrolls again. A cooking clip. A travel reel. A podcast snippet about discipline. Behind him, the barbell is waiting on the rack.

He puts the phone in his pocket and locks it after two minutes. For the following set, he moves ahead.

Pause. Up. Down.

His muscles are entirely capable, although the movement feels a little heavier now. He racks the bar, finishes the reps, and lets out another breath.

Around him, others move with visible intensity. A man several platforms over grunts loudly through a heavy deadlift. On a treadmill, a lady runs with her hair pulled back and her eyes set forward, as like she is sprinting in the direction of something.

In between sets, Aarav stands with a steady breath and an increased but unstrained pulse. He does not feel weak. He does not feel strong. He feels active.

He has been a member of this gym for over four years.

Initially, there was a distinct sense of advancement with every visit. The weights increased steadily. Movements that once felt impossible became routine. Physical changes appeared in the mirror week by week — broader shoulders, thicker arms, posture subtly altered by new strength.

Improvement was visible, measurable, undeniable.

Now the numbers on the bar fluctuate within a narrow range. Some days he lifts slightly more. Some days are slightly less. Over months, the average remains almost unchanged.

Maintenance has replaced momentum.

He does not consciously aim for maintenance. He still arrives with the vague intention to improve. But improvement requires a level of sustained discomfort he rarely pursues to its full extent.

Between sets, his phone reappears almost automatically.

A notification. A quick reply. A glance at something unrelated. Enough time passes for his muscles to cool slightly before he returns to the bar.

The workout stretches longer without becoming harder.

When he leaves the gym he feels like he has accomplished something. He had a better physique and sweaty clothing. His muscles also felt slightly tired.

However, there's no longer the deeper feeling that came with actual effort. He cannot name what is missing. Only that the session felt more like activity than effort.

Drive is less about intensity than direction sustained over time.

Constant stimulation distributes desire across multiple targets simultaneously. Messages, news alerts, short videos, and social updates each present themselves as potentially meaningful.

Every small novelty produces a brief reward signal, training the brain to treat many unrelated inputs as equally relevant. Instead of one dominant objective organizing behavior, attention is pulled toward dozens of minor possibilities.

None persists long enough to establish priority. Motivation becomes diffuse — not absent, but divided into fragments too small to sustain prolonged effort. In earlier environments, options were limited and feedback slower.

Choosing one direction necessarily excluded others, allowing desire to consolidate through constraint. In contrast, abundant stimulation keeps alternative paths continuously visible, preventing commitment from fully stabilizing around any single pursuit.

Sustained effort also begins to feel disproportionately costly when the nervous system is conditioned to rapid rewards.

Activities such as scrolling provide reinforcement every few seconds with minimal discomfort. By comparison, meaningful tasks often require extended periods of uncertainty, frustration, or physical strain before producing any payoff.

In the gym, pushing a set near muscular failure demands thirty to sixty seconds of escalating discomfort with no immediate reward beyond the knowledge that the effort may matter later. The brain implicitly compares these options.

When low-effort stimulation is constantly available, the perceived cost of sustained exertion increases even if the objective difficulty has not changed.

What once felt manageable now registers as unusually taxing, encouraging premature disengagement. This shift reflects recalibration rather than a loss of character or discipline.

Over time, these dynamic favors maintenance over progression. Growth requires repeated cycles of focused strain that accumulate toward structural change — stronger muscles, deeper expertise, expanded capacity.

Such accumulation depends on continuity. When attention resets frequently due to interruptions or self-initiated distraction, each effort episode remains isolated, insufficient to produce meaningful adaptation.

Maintenance, however, demands far less coherence. One can show up, perform familiar routines, and preserve existing capabilities even while mentally elsewhere. Divided attention is compatible with stability but incompatible with advancement.

As a result, activity continues while trajectory flattens. The person remains functional, even productive by conventional standards, yet the underlying system no longer generates forward momentum toward demanding goals.

At work, he is reliable. Tasks assigned to him are completed on schedule. Meetings are attended. Emails are answered with professional politeness.

His performance reviews describe him as "consistent" and "easy to work with."

No one describes him as exceptional.

What is often described as "masculine energy" is, at its core, sustained outward-directed effort — the capacity to apply energy toward goals that resist completion over extended periods.

Although culturally associated with men, this drive is not biologically exclusive to them; it reflects a broader human ability to tolerate difficulty in pursuit of delayed outcomes.

When functioning well, it produces visible progress. When it weakens, the change is subtle. Responsibilities are still met, routines maintained, and life continues to appear stable from the outside.

The difference emerges not in immediate collapse but in the gradual loss of forward momentum.

When it falters, the absence is harder to detect. Nothing collapses immediately. The person continues working, earning, participating.

Only the trajectory flattens.Aarav moves to another machine and adjusts the weight stack.

He performs a set of controlled repetitions, muscles contracting and releasing in a familiar rhythm. Halfway through, his attention drifts. He begins thinking about a presentation scheduled for next week, then about whether he should order groceries tonight or tomorrow.

By the final repetition, he realizes he has not been fully present for most of the set.

He releases the handles and reaches for his phone again.

He switches back to Instagram. Desire has not diminished in Aarav's life. If anything, it has multiplied.

He wants to be healthy, financially secure, socially connected, intellectually engaged. He wants experiences, competence, comfort, novelty.

The problem is not the absence of desire but the absence of consolidation. Each aim pulls in a slightly different direction, none dominant enough to organize the others. Every option remains visible, making exclusive commitment feel premature.

As a result, energy disperses across possibilities rather than concentrating on a single trajectory, producing constant movement without decisive progress.

Across the gym floor, a younger man loads plates onto a bar with visible determination. His movements are sharp, purposeful, almost impatient. When he lifts, his entire body strains against the weight as if something important depends on the outcome.

Aarav watches briefly.

He keeps watching longer than he intends to. The younger man adjusts the plates with quick, economical movements, as if every second matters. There is no hesitation in him, no visible negotiation with discomfort.

When he steps under the bar, his posture changes — not just bracing for weight, but committing to it. The lift is messy, strained, almost reckless, yet unmistakably sincere.

Aarav feels a faint tightness in his chest, unexpected and difficult to place. He remembers being nineteen, staying late in a nearly empty campus gym, adding weight he was not yet strong enough to control simply because improvement felt urgent.

Back then, effort carried the assumption that something important depended on it — not a specific outcome, just a general sense that time was limited and potential perishable.

He tries to identify when that feeling disappeared and cannot. There was no single decision to become cautious, no clear moment of surrender.

It seems to have dissolved gradually, replaced by a quieter logic that prioritizes sustainability over strain.

The younger man finishes his set and steps away, breathing hard, eyes unfocused with effort. He does not notice Aarav watching.

The intensity that filled the space around him dissipates almost immediately, leaving only another ordinary gym member resetting the bar.

Aarav turns back to his own station. The weight on his bar has not changed, but it feels heavier than before, not from fatigue, but from comparison.

There will always be another year to get stronger, another opportunity to advance, another chance to start properly when conditions align.

Urgency dissolves into maintenance.

Women often experience a parallel erosion of momentum, though it is framed less as a loss of drive and more as pressure to succeed across multiple domains simultaneously.

Professional competence, physical fitness, social presence, emotional availability, creative fulfillment, and long-term security are all presented as baseline expectations rather than trade-offs.

Digital environments intensify this pressure: each scroll reveals someone excelling in a different area, making comparison ambient and continuous.

The result is not inactivity but diffusion — energy distributed across too many fronts to produce decisive advancement in any single one.

This produces a pattern similar to Aarav's: constant motion without trajectory. Tasks are completed, responsibilities met, appearances maintained, yet progress feels incremental and fragile because attention cannot remain concentrated long enough for compounding gains. Unlike overt burnout, the state is often externally successful and internally unsatisfying.

The underlying mechanism is shared. When effort is fragmented by competing demands and persistent comparison, forward movement gives way to equilibrium.

Life remains busy, functional, even impressive from the outside, while the sense of directed growth quietly diminishes.

Aarav finishes his workout and walks toward the locker room.

His muscles feel worked but not depleted. His breathing has returned to normal. Sweat cools quickly on his skin, leaving a faint chill in the conditioned air.

He showers, dresses, and checks his reflection briefly before leaving.

He looks healthy. Composed. Entirely functional.

No visible sign of deficiency.

Outside, evening has settled into a soft blue-gray. Traffic moves steadily along the main road, headlights forming continuous streams of light.

Aarav considers walking home instead of taking a cab. The distance is manageable, the weather mild.

He begins walking.

For the first few minutes, the motion feels pleasant — muscles loose, air cool against his face. His thoughts wander without settling.

Then his hand drifts toward his pocket.

The phone emerges.

A notification. A quick glance. A short video begins playing before he consciously decides to watch it. He continues walking, eyes alternating between the sidewalk and the screen.

The video ends. Another begins.

Pedestrians pass around him, adjusting their paths slightly to avoid collision. He remains dimly aware of them, as one remains aware of background noise.

By the time he looks up fully, he is already near his apartment building.

He cannot recall most of the walk. Stimulation felt like energy, but nothing accumulated.

In his apartment, he prepares a simple dinner and eats at the kitchen counter.

The television plays quietly in the background. His phone rests beside the plate, screen lighting intermittently with notifications he checks between bites.

Afterward, he opens a personal certification course he began months earlier, once important for his career. The dashboard shows his progress stalled at 38%.

He starts a lecture and follows it for several minutes before his phone vibrates. A message, then another notification. He checks them reflexively, intending only a brief glance.

When he returns to the laptop, the lecture has advanced beyond what he remembers. He rewinds, tries to reengage, and feels the effort required to reconstruct the argument. The resistance seems disproportionate to the task.

“I’ll do this properly this weekend,” he decides, closing the laptop. The reasoning feels sensible — better to devote focused time later than continue half-attentively now. The apartment grows quiet.

Without tasks or screens demanding attention, a faint restlessness emerges — not anxiety, not boredom, something closer to unspent capacity.

He sits on the couch, hands loosely clasped, unsure what action would satisfy the sensation.

Earlier in his life, this feeling often preceded decisive movement: starting a project, initiating a conversation, going somewhere unfamiliar.

Now it lingers without converting into action. After a few minutes, he picks up his phone. Near midnight, Aarav stands by his bedroom window looking out over the city.

Lights glow in hundreds of windows across neighboring buildings, each one containing a life he cannot see. Cars move below in steady streams, people returning home from places unknown to him.

The scale of it all produces a momentary vertigo — the sense that countless trajectories are unfolding simultaneously, intersecting briefly, diverging again.

He wonders, not for the first time, whether his own trajectory is visible from the outside or indistinguishable from background motion.

He has done many things. Learned skills. Earned money. Maintained relationships. Improved his health.

Yet the narrative thread connecting these efforts feels thin, almost optional.

If he continued exactly as he is for the next five years, the outcome would likely be comfortable, stable, unremarkable.

Aarav lies down and turns off the light.

In the darkness, the room feels larger, edges dissolving into shadow. For a moment he listens to his own breathing, slow and even.

There is no crisis pressing on him. No failure demanding correction. No external force insisting he change course.

Only a faint, persistent sense that something essential is being underutilized — like an engine idling indefinitely, consuming fuel without moving the vehicle.

He closes his eyes. Sleep arrives gradually. On the nightstand, the phone remains silent, inches from his hand. Nothing has gone wrong. Nothing, in particular, is moving forward.

Chapter 6 — The Trap Phase

Why Insight Doesn't Free You

Aarav deletes Instagram at 7:03 a.m.

He trembles for a time until the symbol disappears, leaving his home screen with a small, apparently cleaner blank space. He looks about as if something else, like compulsion, restlessness, or the low-grade anxiety that had been plaguing his days, would vanish along with it.

Nothing changes.

Like putting down something that may otherwise roll back toward him, he carefully locks the phone and sets it face down on the kitchen counter. Coffee brews. The blinds let in slender, uncaring bands of morning light.

He tells himself this is not dramatic. Just an experiment. A reset.

Last night he read an article about attention fragmentation and reward pathways. That's exactly how his evenings had been. He opened an app and scrolled for some time. Later, he closed it, but picked it up again minutes later.

The realization brought a quick flash of clarity — not dread or sadness, just the feeling that something obvious had finally been recognized.

Insight felt like leverage.

Deleting the app felt like action.

By 7:11 a.m., he checks his phone again.

No alerts. His attention is instantly drawn to the empty area where the symbol formerly was, much like a tooth that the tongue keeps going back to. His thumb lingers over it, does not apply any pressure, and then moves away.

Thirty seconds later, he unlocks the phone once more. Email. Weather. Calendar. None hold him. He locks the screen. The sound was drowned out by the absence.

His hand keeps reaching for the phone on the train to work, only to come across his home screen's changing environment each time. He launches a news app, scans over the headlines without reading them, and then shuts it. launches an app for shopping. Closes it. Checks messages that contain nothing new.

Without the familiar feed, his attention skids across substitutes, unable to gain traction. Deleting one outlet has not reduced the impulse to seek stimulation. It has only removed the most efficient route.

A dull pressure accumulated behind his eyes by midmorning. It was not quite a headache, more like cognitive thirst. Work tasks feel unusually dry.

Emails require effort disproportionate to their content. He completes them anyway, slowly, conscientiously.

At lunch, coworkers talk around him. He participates when addressed, nods, offers brief responses. Between exchanges, his hand returns to the phone as if expecting the missing app to have reappeared on its own.

It hasn't.

Someone laughs at a video on their screen across the table. The sound is short, sharp, contagious. Aarav glances up reflexively, then back down at his own empty display.

He feels not deprived exactly, but excluded from a channel of low-effort engagement everyone else still has open.

By late afternoon, work stress begins to accumulate in the ordinary way — deadlines compressing, a request from his manager marked "urgent," a minor mistake that requires correction. Nothing catastrophic. Just friction.

These moments typically turn into brief scrolling stops, little escapes that uplift his mood without necessitating reflection. Today, the strain is rising silently since nothing is taking it away.

He feels extreme stress in his body as he leaves the office at 5:42 p.m. Static that hasn't been released was like this.

While walking home, he uses the App Store.

He does not search immediately. He scrolls featured apps first, as if browsing could conceal intention even from himself. Productivity tools. Language learning platforms. Meditation programs with soft pastel icons promising calm.

None address the specific restlessness vibrating under his skin. He taps the search bar. Types “Instagram.”

Instantly, the app shows up as a recognizable symbol that is comfortingly unaltered. His thumb lingers over the download button long enough to give the impression that he is deliberating.

This is just to check messages, he tells himself. There might be something important. I won’t reinstall it permanently.

He taps.

The progress circle fills with quiet efficiency. Within seconds, the icon returns to its former position, as if it had never left.

Relief arrives before the download finishes.

When the app opens, the feed resumes midstream — same accounts, same tone, same endless scroll. Nothing dramatic happens. No surge of pleasure. Just the subtle easing of pressure, like loosening a tight collar.

The nervous system registers resolution. He lets go without realizing he was holding his breath.

Aarav holds his phone up against a jar in the kitchen while preparing supper that night. Continuous short films with voices overlaying the pan's hiss are played. He watches without full attention, glancing up and down, absorbing fragments rather than content.

When the meal is ready, he eats standing, eyes still on the screen. The stimulation no longer feels rewarding. It feels stabilizing, like background noise preventing something else from becoming audible.

Across the city, Meera lies on her bed with her phone inches from her face, the room dark except for the blue-white glow illuminating her features.

An hour earlier, she deleted TikTok after realizing she had spent most of the evening scrolling instead of finishing a report due tomorrow.

For twenty minutes she stared at the ceiling, restless but determined, the unfinished task open on her laptop nearby.

Then she installed the app again.

Her reasoning was different but structurally identical: I’ll just watch for a few minutes to relax, then I’ll work better.

Now forty-seven minutes have passed. The report remains untouched. Each video produces a small flicker of engagement, none strong enough to justify stopping, none satisfying enough to feel complete.

She is aware of the contradiction the entire time.

Aarav finishes eating and carries the plate to the sink, phone still in his other hand. The video ends. Another begins automatically. He watches it, then another, posture slightly slumped, expression neutral.

At 8:16 p.m., he notices he has reinstalled not only Instagram but also Twitter, which he had deleted weeks earlier after deciding it made him "angry for no reason." He does not remember the exact moment he downloaded it again.

The realization produces a brief flash of self-disgust, sharp but shallow. He considers deleting both apps immediately. Instead, he opens one.

Scrolling feels different now — less like discovery, more like compulsion without narrative. Posts blur together, none retained long enough to matter.

He is not searching for information or connection, only maintaining the flow.

Stress earlier in the day has paired itself with stimulation as the expected antidote.

Breaking the chain requires tolerating the discomfort without immediate discharge, a skill rarely practiced in environments where escape is always available.

When psychologists describe habits, they often reduce them to a simple loop: cue → routine → reward. The cue is a trigger — internal or external — that signals the brain to initiate a familiar pattern.

The routine is the behavior itself. The reward is not necessarily pleasure; it is whatever change in state the brain learns to expect afterward. Over time, the loop compresses into an automatic sequence executed with minimal conscious input.

Crucially, this process operates largely below awareness. The brain systems that encode well-learned habits — particularly circuits involving the basal ganglia — are designed for efficiency, not deliberation.

Once a pattern has been repeated enough times, it can run faster than reflective thought produced by the prefrontal cortex. Intention arrives late, like a narrator trying to explain a decision that has already been made.

This is why insight alone rarely produces change. Understanding a habit recruits conscious reasoning, but the habit itself is initiated elsewhere, often milliseconds after the cue appears.

By the time awareness registers the urge, the behavioral pathway is already active. Stopping it requires effortful inhibition, which is metabolically costly and therefore difficult to sustain, especially under fatigue or stress.

In Aarav's case, the cue is not the app itself but the internal state that precedes it: tension, boredom, uncertainty, the low hum of unresolved demands. The routine is reaching for stimulation — unlocking the phone, reinstalling, scrolling.

The reward is relief, subtle but reliable: a reduction in friction, a temporary narrowing of attention, the quieting of background unease. Each successful pass through the loop strengthens the expectation that this sequence will work again.

Importantly, the brain does not evaluate whether the outcome is meaningful or beneficial in the long term. It only registers that the unpleasant state diminished. From a learning perspective, the loop is successful.

Awareness that the behavior is unproductive does not erase the circuitry that has already been reinforced through repetition.

Over time, the sequence becomes less about seeking enjoyment and more about avoiding discomfort. The routine persists not because it feels good, but because not performing it feels worse.

A second process compounds this pattern: stress and stimulation become neurologically paired through repetition. When relief consistently follows exposure to fast, engaging content, the brain begins to associate one with the other.

Structures involved in emotional learning, such as the amygdala, encode this contingency quickly and efficiently. Eventually, the presence of stress alone is enough to generate a craving for stimulation, even before conscious thought evaluates options.

This pairing operates automatically. The body registers tension — elevated heart rate, muscle tightness, diffuse unease — and predicts the action that previously reduced it.

The urge does not feel like a learned response; it feels like a need arising spontaneously. Because the relief is immediate and the cost delayed, the conditioned pathway dominates decision-making in the moment.

Deleting the app removes the tool but not the association. The underlying linkage between discomfort and digital engagement remains intact, waiting for any available substitute or opportunity to reactivate the cycle. Reinstallation, in this context, is not a fresh choice so much as the completion of an interrupted pattern.

Willpower struggles because it operates intermittently, while conditioning operates continuously. As long as stress continues to occur — which it inevitably does — the paired response will continue to surface. Each repetition further stabilizes the expectation that stimulation is the fastest route back to equilibrium.

Seen this way, relapse is less a dramatic failure than a predictable outcome of intact learning systems functioning exactly as designed.

Meera finally sits up, alarmed by the time. She opens her laptop, reads the first paragraph of her report, and feels the cognitive effort required to reenter the task.

Her phone vibrates beside her.

She checks it instantly.

A notification from the same app she intended to avoid — new videos, new messages, new proof that the stream has continued without her. The unfinished report feels heavier by comparison, dense with effort and uncertainty.

She returns to scrolling.

Not because she prefers it, but because it is easier to continue than to switch.

By midnight, Aarav is back on his couch, posture nearly identical to the previous night. The television plays unheard. His phone illuminates his face from below, casting faint shadows under his eyes.

He remembers deleting the app that morning. The memory feels distant, almost theoretical, like recalling a plan that belonged to someone else. He could delete it again right now. The thought passes without action.

Part of him understands that tomorrow will likely repeat the same sequence: resolve, removal, gradual pressure, reinstatement.

Relapse becomes routine rather than dramatic.

He tells himself he will be more disciplined when work is less stressful, when he sleeps better, when something external shifts. Each condition feels reasonable, postponing change without explicitly rejecting it.

The Trap Phase thrives on indefinite deferral.

Across town, Meera closes the app at last, not out of satisfaction but exhaustion. The report deadline looms unchanged.

She sets an alarm to wake early and finish it before work, a plan she has executed many times before with mixed success.

Her phone remains in her hand as she falls asleep.

Insight has not failed because it was weak. It has failed because the environment continues to supply immediate alternatives that require no negotiation, no planning, no vulnerability.

Awareness alone does not remove access.

At 12:38 a.m., Aarav finally locks his phone and places it on the coffee table. The room expands into silence, thick and unfamiliar.

Without the steady stream of input, residual thoughts begin surfacing — fragments of the day, unresolved concerns, a vague sense of time passing without accumulation.

He feels suddenly tired, not from exertion but from low-grade engagement sustained for hours. For a moment, he considers moving the phone to another room.

He doesn't.

Keeping it nearby preserves the option of relief if the quiet becomes uncomfortable. The possibility is enough; he does not need to act on it immediately.

This, too, is part of the trap: the device functions as both stimulus and reassurance, a portable exit from any internal state that becomes too pronounced.

He turns off the lights and lies down on the couch instead of going to bed, unsure why. The apartment hums softly — refrigerator, distant traffic, the faint buzz of electricity through unseen wiring.

Nothing is wrong.

Nothing feels resolved.

Morning will bring another attempt, another deletion, another belief that understanding should translate into control. The cycle will reset not because he wants it to, but because the forces sustaining it remain unchanged.

On the table beside him, the phone screen lights briefly with a notification, then fades. Aarav watches the glow disappear without reaching for it, a small victory so fragile it barely registers.

He closes his eyes.

In the darkness, one recognition remains, clear and unwelcome: he is not trapped because he cannot see the cage. He is trapped because the door is open, and he keeps walking back inside.

Chapter 7 — The Guilt Loop

When Coping Turns Inward

At almost midnight Aarav decides to clear his browser history.

He does it quickly and almost ceremonially. Three taps. Confirm. The list disappears, leaving a blank screen that feels cleaner than it is.

For a few seconds, he does nothing.

The room is dimly lit by his screen, and his laptop hums lightly on his thighs. The city has faded to irregular headlights that pass by his curtains like some distant clouds.

Rather than being a signal of effort, his calm breathing is a sign of alertness. It seems as though his body has not yet been informed that the encounter is over. He opens the laptop again after closing it halfway.

The ensuing hush is thick and instantaneous. There are no abrupt visual shifts or audio leaks from the speakers.

His phone on the coffee table flashes a notice for a moment before going black. He doesn't grab for it. Instead, he looks at the blank laptop lid. Uninvited and fully formed, a thought comes to him: Why did I just do it again?

The query has no solution ready for it.

He thinks someone might come in. Anyone. A stranger. A friend. Doesn’t really matter.

His face feels warm. He looks around for a second. Like he forgot something. Or missed it.

His hands just hang there between his knees. He’s looking at the floor. Leaning forward a bit. Waiting, I guess. For something. Not clear what.

He stays like that. Too long, probably. Then he gets up. Takes the laptop to the bedroom. Leaves it on the desk.

Later he goes back. Not to bed. Just the living room.
Turns off the lamp. Falls asleep on the couch.

Although he cannot explain why, sleep feels useless.

With her back to the cabinet door, Meera is seated on the bathroom floor across the city with her phone in her hand and its screen blank.

Although she hasn't been sobbing, there is a slight burning in her eyes as though she was going to cry but stopped herself.

She had been watching a number of videos that featured strangers discussing their concerns in front of cameras, lifestyle advice, and romance advice. With each tape offering insight on loneliness, self-worth, attachment, and healing, the content steadily changed algorithmically.

She watched them all.

Not with curiosity. With compulsion.

When the final video ended, the next one began automatically. She closed the app abruptly, as if cutting a wire.

The silence starts to press in while she sits on the cold tile.

Her reflection in the dark mirror above the sink looks off. Not distorted—just… distant. Like it isn't really her. Like someone else is wearing her face.

A single thought loops, phrased less as language than as tone:

Something is wrong with me.

She unlocks her phone and opens the same app again, then stops before the feed loads. The impulse feels less like desire than like gravitational pull.

If she resumes, the feeling will be dull. She knows this from experience.

She locks the screen instead.

The quick, temporary relief is followed by a more intense recurrence of the ache she was attempting to ease. Without healing the wound, avoidance has eliminated the anesthetic.

Her shoulders tense. She pulls her knees in, curling in on herself a little. Like that might help. Somehow.

Most people think of guilt as something useful. From a subjective perspective, it feels like betrayal by one's own mind.

It should help.
It should fix something.
It doesn't.

A signal.
You messed up. Fix it.
Sometimes that works.

But when everything already feels like too much—
it stops working.

It comes back.
Then again.
And again.

Nothing changes.

Behavior creates discomfort.
Discomfort turns into guilt.

Guilt makes the discomfort louder.
Louder discomfort pushes the same behavior.

The loop closes.
Then tightens.

The target shifts.
Not the world—you.

You can't step away from yourself.
There's nowhere to go.

This is where numbing behaviors gain disproportionate power. They do not solve the underlying issue; they temporarily reduce the intensity of self-perception.

The loop doesn't just repeat. It turns inward.

At 1:26 a.m., Aarav is still awake. His body is tired, but his mind remains hyper-alert in a directionless way, scanning for thoughts to resolve.

Fragments of the evening replay out of sequence — not the content itself, but the decision points. The moment he opened the laptop. The hesitation that lasted less than a second. The quiet awareness that he could stop and did not.

He considers opening his phone to distract himself, then rejects the idea almost reflexively. More input feels intolerable, like adding noise to an already saturated channel.

What he wants is not stimulation but absolution, though he would not use that word. His gaze settles on the ceiling, tracking faint patterns in the paint. A subtler thought emerges beneath the self-criticism: If I were different, this wouldn't happen.

Different how remains unspecified — stronger, more disciplined, less lonely, less impulsive, more mature.

The body responds to this belief as if to defeat. His muscles loosen not into relaxation but into slackness, energy draining rather than settling.

He turns onto his side, facing the back of the couch, folding inward again.

Sleep finally arrives not as rest but as shutdown.

Meera returns to her bedroom and sits on the edge of the bed without turning on the light.

Her laptop is open to a document she had intended to work on earlier. The cursor blinks patiently at the end of an unfinished sentence, unchanged since the evening began.

She reads the paragraph from the start, comprehension sluggish, as if her cognitive bandwidth has been partially depleted.

She closes the laptop without saving. Out of quiet resignation that tonight will not be productive in any domain.

Lying down, she turns onto her side and pulls the blanket up to her chin despite the room being warm. The gesture is instinctive, protective rather than functional.

Her phone rests on the nightstand within reach. She places her hand over it, not picking it up, just confirming its presence.

Knowing she could escape reduces the urgency to do so immediately. Gradually, her breathing slows. Just before sleep, a final thought surfaces with unexpected clarity: I don't even know what I was trying to feel.

It turns inward.
The same thought loops.
The same guilt returns.

Morning arrives without ceremony.

Aarav wakes on the couch with a stiff neck and a dry mouth, disoriented for a few seconds before memory reassembles. Sunlight filters through the curtains, neutral and indifferent.

His first impulse is to stand and begin the day immediately, as if forward motion might outrun recollection.

The heaviness is lighter but still present, like residue after a spill has been wiped up.

Before moving, he notices something else. A quiet resolve forming, familiar in its phrasing: Tonight will be different.

The statement contains no plan, no strategy, no acknowledgment of the conditions that produced the previous night. It functions less as a commitment than as a psychological reset button, allowing him to proceed without fully integrating the experience.

He stands. In the kitchen, water boils, coffee grounds bloom, the routine reasserting itself with comforting predictability. From the outside, nothing appears disrupted.

The loop persists because relief is immediate and change is not.

Guilt then enters as both consequence and amplifier.

From a learning perspective, the loop is coherent.

It still feels like betrayal.

Breaking the cycle requires a capacity rarely cultivated in high-stimulation contexts: remaining present with unresolved internal states without immediately modifying them.

Not solving.
Not suppressing.
Not distracting.

Enduring.

That evening, Aarav sits at his desk with the laptop closed in front of him. He has not opened it since morning.

The urge is present but diffuse, more like pressure than direction. Nothing compels action strongly enough to override hesitation. The apartment is quiet. Too quiet.

For a moment, he considers leaving — going for a walk, calling someone, inventing an errand. Instead, he stays seated, hands resting on the desk, eyes unfocused.

The discomfort builds gradually, cresting without breaking. Then something unusual happens. It stabilizes. The pressure does not kill him.

It does not even incapacitate him. It just feels uncomfortable. A small, unexpected realization surfaces: The feeling he had been trying to eliminate was survivable.

Across the city, Meera stands at her bedroom window watching traffic move below, phone on the dresser behind her. She feels restless, unsatisfied, vaguely exposed. This time, she does nothing. Cars pass. Lights change.

Gradually, the urgency dissolves into something quieter, less sharp. Not contentment. Not clarity. Just the absence of acute pressure.

She turns away from the window and prepares for bed without checking the phone. Neither of them feels triumphant. Only a subtle shift.

This does not erase the loop. It does not guarantee future resistance. But it introduces a competing memory: that escape is not the only possible outcome. In the darkness, Aarav lies in bed, eyes open. He does not chase them. He does not suppress them. He waits.

Eventually, sleep comes — slower than sedation, quieter than collapse. Just before drifting off, a final recognition forms, sharper than the night before:

The room remains silent. Nothing external has changed. For the first time, the absence of noise does not feel like an accusation. It feels like space.

Chapter 8 — Motivation Fatigue

When Work Becomes Unrewarding

Aarav opens his laptop at 9:12 a.m. and examines the duties that are waiting for him. He notices just three things, all of which are familiar.

All of which are also doable, and none of which requires him to do anything new.

He reads the first one slowly, then again, as if repetition might trigger the impulse to begin. It does not.

He knows that nothing is truly preventing him as he sits there with his hands softly resting on the keyboard.

There is no conflicting demand, no urgency elsewhere, and no distraction grabbing his attention.

The absence of resistance should make starting easier. Instead, it makes the stillness more noticeable.

He takes a few deep breaths and corrects his posture, a tiny bodily reset he has performed many times. Then he starts typing, carefully and precisely recording a few sentences.

The motion feels right, yet it feels oddly unsupported, as if it were started without any momentum.

He pauses and reads his writing again after a little while. He finds it okay with nothing wrong about it. Nevertheless, he removes the line and allows his hands to return to their original positions.

He is not irritated; rather, he is not persuaded that continuing would feel any different.

The workplace continues uninterrupted around him. Keyboards clack in constant beats, people switch between workstations, and conversations come and go.

Everything appears normal, including him, which makes the lack of internal movement harder to justify.

He opens a second tab, not to escape but to check something briefly. Then another. The transitions don't announce themselves. They are insignificant enough to ignore, yet they mount up and push him away from the work without ever seeming like a choice.

It's odd when he returns to the initial screen; it feels like he's in a place he never quite reached. The pointer continues to flash steadily, as it waits for something that never truly began.

With a sigh, he reclines. Later, he seems to be finishing up a chat before it finishes by lowering the laptop halfway. He doesn't question the delay, even if it doesn't seem reasonable.

Meera is sitting at her workstation with a notepad open across the city. The page is empty, mostly—just a heading from a few minutes ago, underlined a little too carefully.

She already knows what should come next. The structure's there, the points are clear. It's not confusion holding her up.

She lifts her pen, hesitates. The first sentence almost forms—close enough to feel—but then it's gone before she can pin it down.

Holding onto it takes more effort than it should. Just enough to make her stop trying.

She puts down the pen and reclines, her gaze straying to the window. It's simpler to monitor the continuous flow of cars below than whatever her thoughts are doing.

After a minute, she gets up and goes to the kitchen. Fills the kettle. Switches it on. No hesitation there.

These small things run on their own, unlike the larger task waiting for her.

When she comes back, the page hasn't changed. The heading feels heavier now, as if it is subtly anticipating something from her, even if it is still tidy and composed.

She takes the pen and sits down once again. This time, she pauses in the middle of the second phrase and writes a short line.

Although the statements are accurate, no one is inspired to keep going by them.

She gently shuts the notepad, not because she's frustrated but more because she doesn't exactly understand why it seems useless to continue.

The person is not blocked. The pathway is visible. What's missing is the internal reinforcement that usually sustains movement once it begins.

Meera decides to approach her work differently. Instead of writing full sentences, she begins outlining ideas in short fragments, hoping that reducing the effort required will help her maintain momentum.

The first few points come easily. For a little while, it seems as though the strategy is working as she rapidly and seemingly instinctively writes them down.

The brain starts to modify how it assesses effort when it regularly results in delayed or muted rewards.

Once-neutral or manageable tasks begin to register as somewhat more expensive—not in terms of difficulty, but in terms of what they now yield.

Nothing about the task itself changes. The shift occurs in the expectation surrounding it.

The brain begins to lean toward experiences that respond immediately, even if they require less depth.

Over time, this creates a subtle imbalance—effort starts to feel disproportionately heavy, not because the task has changed, but because it no longer competes with faster, more accessible rewards.

Attention fragments more easily, and engagement becomes shallower, often fading before it has the chance to stabilize.

As this recalibration settles in, starting remains possible, but sustaining effort becomes less automatic. A tiny, purposeful push is now required with every step—something that was not before present.

The time is 2:37 p.m. Aarav finally makes the much anticipated call. He speaks in a composed and professional manner. To anyone listening, it would sound entirely routine.

Nothing in his voice gives anything away. There's no strain, no hesitation you could point to.

The conversation itself stays easy, almost uneventful. No tension rises, no sharp turns—just a smooth exchange that moves forward without resistance. He asks the right questions, takes notes, and moves through the discussion with quiet competence.

When the call ends, he remains seated for a moment, phone still in his hand. There is no sense of relief or completion, only the absence of the task that had been there before.

He places the phone down and looks back at his laptop. One task remains.

He does not open it.

Meera opens her laptop and returns to the document she had left unfinished earlier. The cursor blinks at the same point, unchanged, waiting for continuation.

She scrolls up and rereads the previous section, trying to reconnect with the mindset she had while writing it. The content makes sense, but the mental state feels distant, like something she can observe but not fully reenter.

She begins typing a sentence, then stops midway and deletes it. The second attempt follows the same pattern, slightly different words leading to the same quiet halt.

The process repeats, not rapidly, but with enough consistency to prevent any real momentum from forming.

She is working, in the technical sense. The document is open, the effort is present, but nothing is accumulating.

By early evening, Aarav has completed everything he needed to do. Each task is finished to an acceptable standard, and there is no external reason to consider the day unproductive.

Still, the experience of it feels strangely incomplete. Not exhausting, not satisfying, just flat in a way that is difficult to define.

He closes his laptop and remains seated for a moment longer than necessary. Normally, finishing work creates a subtle shift, a sense of transition into the rest of the day.

Today, there is no clear boundary. Work has ended, but nothing has replaced it.

Meera lies on her bed with her laptop beside her, the document now complete. She reads through the final paragraph once more, confirming that it does what it needs to do.

It does.

She closes the file and sets the laptop aside. There is no sense of closure, no internal acknowledgment that something has been completed.

Her phone rests within reach, but she does not pick it up immediately. For a few seconds, she simply lies there, looking at the ceiling, aware of a quiet absence where a feeling of completion would normally be.

Motivation fatigue does not arrive as a sudden loss of discipline. It develops gradually, through repeated exposure to environments where effort is optional and reward is immediate.

Over time, the system adjusts. The baseline for what feels engaging shifts, and tasks that once required little effort to begin now demand a level of initiation that feels slightly out of proportion.

Nothing breaks. Everything continues to function.

Only the underlying drive begins to thin out.

At 8:14 p.m., Aarav sits at his desk again, not because he has to, but because he feels like he should. The laptop is closed in front of him, and his hands rest lightly on the surface of the desk.

For a while, he does nothing. There is no distraction, no immediate urge to escape the quiet. Just the presence of the moment and the awareness that he could start something if he chose to.

The thought forms slowly. Not a plan, not a clear intention, just the recognition that action is still available to him.

He opens the laptop.

The screen lights up, and he hesitates briefly before selecting something small. A task simple enough that it should not require much effort.

He begins.

The first few seconds feel heavier than expected, as if the act of starting carries more resistance than it should. He continues anyway, moving slowly, one line at a time.

There is no surge of motivation, no sudden clarity or momentum. Only the quiet continuation of effort, sustained without reinforcement.

After a minute, something shifts slightly. The resistance does not disappear, but it stabilizes, becoming something he can move through rather than something that stops him.

Across the city, Meera returns to her desk and opens the notebook once more. The same page is still there, unchanged, waiting for continuation.

She picks up the pen and pauses, expecting the same hesitation to return. It does.

This time, she does not set the pen down.

She writes one sentence, then another, each one carrying a weight that feels slightly disproportionate to its size. There is no satisfaction in it, no immediate reward.

She pauses, waiting for the usual disengagement.

It does not come right away.

The discomfort remains, but so does the action.

Effort, in this state, does not feel inherently rewarding. It does not justify itself in the moment or provide immediate feedback that encourages continuation.

It simply becomes something that can be done, even when it does not feel compelling.

Later that night, Aarav lies in bed, staring at the ceiling. The room is quiet, the day behind him complete in every practical sense.

He thinks briefly about the small task he started in the evening, the way it felt heavier than it should have, and the way that weight eventually leveled out without ever becoming easy.

It is not a breakthrough. Not a return to anything he recognizes as drive.

Just a different experience than the rest of the day.

Across the city, Meera closes her notebook and turns off the light. The few lines she wrote sit unfinished, neither significant nor meaningless.

As she lies down, a faint awareness settles in, difficult to define but clear enough to notice.

The effort is still there.

It just doesn’t feel like it used to.

And for now, that is all she can observe.

CHAPTER 9 - The Silent Struggle

It begins as it usually does: the same bar, the same patrons, the same familiar versions of everyone. The kind of place chosen for nostalgia—the type that lets you pretend nothing has really changed, even when it obviously has.

For a while, it works.

Old stories resurface. The same ones, somehow funnier each time. Drinks arrive, phones come out, a few pictures get taken—small rituals that signal everything is fine, everyone is doing well, life is moving in the right direction.

And if you were sitting there, you wouldn't question it either.

You'd laugh at the same moments. Add your own version of a story you've told before. Nod along when someone talks about work or relationships. From the outside, it would feel easy. Familiar.

Normal.

There's a pause.

Not a big one. Most people wouldn't notice it unless they were already paying attention. But if you were there—really there—

you'd feel it. Just for a second. A slight break in rhythm, like something unscripted, almost made it into the conversation.

And then it happens.

Someone laughs. Quick. A bit too quick.

And it's gone in an instant.

"Yes, most likely because you're still unmarried at thirty."

The moment disappears in a matter of seconds as another one heaps on. The conversation continues as if nothing had happened after the man who said it laughs too, maybe louder than is required.

The prior round does not return, and a second round is requested.

You remain longer than you had anticipated, but after that, not much changes. Everyone plays their role without giving it any thought, and the talk continues returning to the same safe subjects. When you go, it appears to be completed in the manner of a routine rather than in the manner of something noteworthy.

The stroll back is quieter than it is at night. No music, no voices, just the persistent, uncomfortable hum in your mind. For a brief time, it seems as though something could emerge now that there is room for it.

It doesn't.

Almost instinctively, your palm lunges for your phone because the quiet seems strange rather than because there is something essential to check. In a matter of seconds, something simpler to interact with takes your focus once more.

By the time you get home, whatever almost came up at the bar is already out of reach.

Nothing about that interaction feels unusual, which is exactly why it matters. No one was trying to shut him down, and no one would even remember it happening. But something real showed up, and the group moved away from it almost instantly.

Not with silence, but with humor.

That's how most conversations work now if you look closely. They're not empty or fake, just carefully managed so nothing slows down or cuts too deep. Everyone participates in keeping it that way.

This begins to seem more like personality than pattern by the time you're in your late twenties or early thirties. You convince yourself that you manage your own affairs, that you're simply private, or that you dislike discussing your issues. It even sounds like strength at first glance.

To be fair, it is frequently handled as such.

You are the one who doesn't complicate things, is dependable, and needs minimal maintenance. You are trusted since you don't generate mayhem in the space. However, most people seldom take the time to assess their level of composure.

The disconnect doesn't arrive all at once. Since nothing is clearly broken, it develops gradually in ways that are simple to overlook.

You still go out, laugh, and get surrounded by people. However, sometimes you feel a little detached from what happens. It is as if you're taking part but not truly engaged.

You answer questions, but your answers are clean and efficient instead of honest. "Yeah, I've been good. Just busy." It's not a lie, but it's also not the truth.

What's changed isn't your ability to talk. It's your ability to feel something clearly enough to put into words.

And that shift doesn't come from nowhere, even if it feels like it did.

Earlier, we talked about dopamine as anticipation, reward, and motivation. But there's another effect that's easier to miss—over time, it starts to narrow your emotional range.

When your baseline is constantly elevated through stimulation, your system adapts by becoming less sensitive. You don't notice it happening because nothing feels dramatically wrong, just slightly muted.

Subtle emotions stop registering as clearly, and discomfort gets bypassed before it has a chance to fully surface. Stillness starts to feel unnecessary, almost inefficient.

And when something feels inefficient, you stop choosing it.

You stop sitting with thoughts that don't resolve quickly. You stop entertaining emotions that don't have a clear outcome. Anything that lingers too long starts to feel like a problem instead of a process.

So you shorten everything.

Attention spans get tighter, conversations get lighter, and your tolerance for anything emotionally complex starts to drop without you noticing it. Not because you decided to avoid depth, but because you've trained yourself to prefer what moves faster.

Over time, depth doesn't disappear—it just starts to feel out of place.

A long day doesn't turn into reflection anymore; it turns into scrolling or background noise. A stressful moment doesn't turn into a conversation; it turns into distraction. Even when something feels off, there's always something easier to reach for.

Video, music, content, porn—whatever works fastest.

Not because you lack discipline, but because the alternative requires more from you. It requires sitting still long enough to actually feel what's going on, and that's a skill that quietly fades when you stop using it.

There are nights where you notice it more clearly.

You're lying in bed, phone in hand, switching between apps without really engaging with any of them. A video plays, then another, then something else replaces it before it even finishes.

Nothing is bad enough to stop.

Nothing is good enough to stay.

You're not even enjoying it, but you're also not putting it down. It fills the space just enough to keep anything else from coming through.

And somewhere in the background, there's a vague awareness that you could be doing something else—thinking, reflecting, even reaching out to someone—but that option feels heavier for no clear reason.

So you stay where it's easy.

Over time, something important gets trained out of you. You lose the ability to stay with your own experience long enough to process it properly.

If you don't process it, you can't articulate it. And if you can't articulate it, you don't share it.

So the silence isn't always a conscious decision. Sometimes, it's just a lack of clarity that you've learned to live with.

It shows up in small, forgettable moments.

You think about texting someone—not for a reason, not to make plans, just to talk. Their name comes to mind, your phone is already in your hand, and for a second, it feels like you might actually do it.

You even open the conversation.

Then you pause.

You don't know what you'd say exactly, and suddenly that matters more than it should. It starts to feel unnecessary, maybe even a little awkward, so you close it and tell yourself you'll do it another time.

You don't.

Not because you made a decision not to, but because the moment passed and nothing pushed you to act on it.

This is where the disconnect deepens.

When you're sitting in that bar and a moment opens up, it's not just that you choose to avoid it. It's that you don't fully know how to go there anymore, and even if you did, you've spent years practicing how not to.

So instead, you rely on what you've gotten good at.

You keep things light, you make people laugh, and you shift attention away from anything that might slow the room down. You say just enough to stay engaged without saying anything that actually exposes you.

This carries into every part of life, especially dating.

You can hold attention and keep things interesting, and you know how to create attraction without much effort. On the surface, everything works.

But when things start to slow down and move toward something real, something that requires presence instead of performance, it feels different. Not wrong, just flatter than expected.

Real connection doesn't spike the way stimulation does. It settles, and if your system is used to constant spikes, that settling can feel like something is missing.

So you pull back, usually in small ways that are easy to justify. You tell yourself the person isn't quite right, or that something feels off, or that you just need more space.

Sometimes that's true.

But sometimes, it's this: you've trained yourself to engage with stimulation, not connection.

The same pattern shows up outside of dating too.

You can spend hours consuming content without noticing the time pass, but struggle to sit through a slow, honest conversation without feeling restless. You can stay engaged when there's constant input, but feel slightly disconnected when things get quiet.

Even around people, there are moments where you feel like you're observing more than participating. You're there, but not fully in it.

So you adapt in a way that looks like growth from the outside.

You become more independent, more self-contained, and less demanding of others. You need less, you expect less, and you keep more of your life to yourself.

And again, this gets rewarded.

No drama, no neediness, no complications. But underneath that, something else is happening—you're slowly removing yourself from experiences that require emotional presence.

At some point, this starts to feel normal, even preferable. You tell yourself you like your space, that you don't need much, that you're good on your own.

Part of that is true.

The other part is harder to admit: you've gotten used to not being fully known.

Because being known requires exposure, and exposure requires clarity. Clarity, in turn, requires sitting with your own experience long enough to understand it.

Which is exactly what your habits have been helping you avoid.

So the silence continues, not because no one cares, but because everyone has learned how to stay just above the surface. It's subtle, automatic, and shared by almost everyone in the room.

Every once in a while, someone dips slightly below it and says something real. Almost immediately, the group pulls it back up with a joke or a shift in tone.

Not intentionally.

Reflexively.

If you start paying attention, you'll notice it happening in real time. Not just in others, but in yourself.

The moment you change the subject slightly too fast. The moment you add humor to take the edge off something real. The moment you give a polished answer instead of an honest one.

Those moments are easy to miss, but they're not random.

They're patterns.

And once you see them, you can't unsee them.

Not all at once, and not in a way that suddenly fixes anything. But enough to recognize that what you've been calling independence might not be what it looks like.

It might just be disconnection, practiced long enough to feel like identity.

Chapter 10 — When Coping Becomes Identity

A few minutes before his alarm goes off, Aarav awakens.

He stays put for a while.

Everything appears shallower than it actually is because the room is dark and the drapes are only partially drawn, let in a faint gray light. He simply dozes off there with his eyes open for a while without giving anything any special thought.

Then he grabs for the nightstand. Not immediately. Really, not even deliberately.

Just something he does.

The screen lights up. Notifications, scattered and unremarkable. Messages he doesn't feel like responding to yet. Updates that don't require attention but hold it anyway.

He scrolls for a bit. Nothing specific. Just enough to ease into the morning.

Ten minutes had gone by before he sits up. Time lost is not recorded. Just a portion of awakening.

Everything goes according to plan in the kitchen. Coffee, the machine's faint hum, the same pattern repeated without any resistance. His phone is leaning on the counter at a slight angle to maintain background music.

He's not watching it. But he's not not watching it either. The space never fully goes quiet.

Across the city, Meera is already at her desk.

Her laptop is open, a document pulled up from the night before. She reads the last few lines, not to edit, just to re-enter the flow of it.

For a few seconds, she considers continuing. Instead, she reaches for her phone. It's a small interruption. Harmless, almost procedural. A quick check before starting.

A message, a video, another one queued immediately after. It doesn't seem like a choice since the change is so seamless.

The paper seems a little farther away than it did a minute ago as she turns back to the screen.

Not difficult. Just less immediate. She tells herself she'll start in a bit. The thought is familiar. There is no longer any urgency to it.

Aarav had already joined a call, replied to emails, and made a list of the tasks for the day before midmorning.

Nothing seems strange from the outside.

He speaks clearly. Listens, when required. Even adds input at the right moments. There's no hesitation you could point to, nothing that suggests anything is missing.

When the call ends, he leans back in his chair, exhaling slowly. There's a brief window where he could move directly into the next task.

He doesn't.

His hand moves to his phone again, almost as a continuation of the pause.

It's not about avoiding work. He'll do it.

Just not immediately.

That gap—small, unremarkable—has started to stretch over time. Not enough to disrupt anything. Just enough to reshape how his day unfolds.

Work happens in segments now. So does everything else.

Meera notices something similar, though she wouldn't describe it that way.

Her day moves, but not in a straight line.

She starts tasks easily enough. It's the middle that slips.

A message here. A short break there. Something quick to reset before continuing.

Each shift feels justified on its own.

When combined, they create a pattern that she no longer questions.

Eventually, she begins to follow the day's schedule rather than choosing it.

Not intentionally.

Just consistently.

This is how coping changes form.

It begins as a response.

Something you reach for when you feel off, overwhelmed, or unsure what to do next. A way to take the edge off, to create a little distance from whatever is building underneath.

Used occasionally, it works.

Used repeatedly, it becomes reliable.

And reliability is what the brain remembers.

Over time, the behavior detaches from the original problem. It no longer requires discomfort to activate. The cue becomes softer, less defined.

A pause.

A transition.

A moment where nothing immediate is happening.

That's enough.

The response fills the space automatically.

Not because something is wrong, but because something could be.

And it's easier to stay ahead of that possibility than to wait and find out.

By evening, Aarav is back home, sitting on the couch with his laptop open.

A show plays in the background. His phone rests beside him, lighting up intermittently. He shifts between them without fully committing to either.

Work is technically done.

There's nothing pressing left.

Still, the sense of completion doesn't arrive.

It rarely does anymore.

So he keeps the input going.

Not chasing anything specific. Just maintaining a certain level of engagement, enough to avoid the drop that comes with stopping completely.

At some point, he notices the overlap—multiple streams, none fully held.

The thought passes quickly.

This is just how he unwinds.

Across the city, Meera turns off her laptop and lies back on her bed.

The room is quiet for a few seconds.

Then she reaches for her phone.

There's no reason this time. No leftover task, no stress she can point to. Just the absence of something to do.

The screen fills it immediately.

Minutes pass. Then more.

The content changes, but the experience doesn't.

Light engagement. Continuous motion. Nothing that requires her to stay.

At one point, she pauses on a video longer than usual. Not because it's better. Just because it holds her attention slightly more than the rest.

When it ends, she feels the shift—subtle, but noticeable. A small drop.

She scrolls again before it can settle.

The adjustment is automatic. This is the part that's easy to miss. Nothing here feels extreme.

There's no clear moment where a line is crossed, no single decision that marks a change. From the outside, everything still looks functional, even balanced.

Work gets done. Messages are answered. Life continues to move. But underneath that, something has reorganized itself. Relief is no longer something you seek occasionally.

It becomes something you maintain. The baseline shifts quietly.

Moments that used to feel neutral now feel incomplete unless they are filled. Silence registers as something to move through rather than something to stay in.

And gradually, without being stated outright, a different understanding takes hold:

This is just how you are.

Not easily bored—just used to stimulation.

Not avoiding anything—just staying occupied.

Not disconnected—just independent.

The language adjusts first.

The behavior follows without resistance.

Aarav closes his laptop around 11:40 p.m. and sits there for a moment, the room finally still.

His phone is within reach. He doesn't pick it up immediately.

For a few seconds, nothing replaces the quiet. It feels unfamiliar. Not uncomfortable, exactly. Just undefined.

He considers getting up, maybe heading to bed, maybe doing something else. The options pass through without settling.

Then the screen beside him lights up. He glances at it. Just a notification. Nothing important. His hand moves anyway.

Across the city, Meera turns onto her side, phone still in her hand, the glow soft against the wall.

Her eyes move, but more slowly now. The content continues. There's no clear stopping point. There doesn't need to be.

At some level, neither of them is trying to escape anything in particular. There's no immediate discomfort pressing in, no sharp emotion demanding relief.

And that's what makes it harder to notice. The behavior remains. Even when the reason is gone. Not as a choice. Not as a reaction. But as something closer to default.

Something that no longer feels separate from who they are.

And because of that, it no longer feels like something that needs to be changed.

Chapter 11 - Why Detox Fails

And Why Rebound Wins

Aarav doesn't decide to quit in a moment of crisis. Nothing breaks sharply enough to force it. The choice develops gradually over the course of nights. However, end without feeling resolved and mornings that seem heavier than they should.

It sounds possible by the time he says it aloud. "I believe I require a reset." Calm, controlled, almost like a logical next step rather than a reaction.

That same night, the idea becomes more defined. Not just cutting back. Not being "more mindful." A clean break. A detox.

He looks it up the way he looks up everything else—quickly, selectively, skimming for certainty. Thirty-day detox. Quit dopamine. Life after scrolling. The language is simple, convincing, structured.

The promise is clear. Remove the noise, and everything returns. Focus, discipline, clarity. As if these things were waiting just beneath the surface, delayed only by access.

What appeals to him isn't just the outcome. It's the sharpness of the approach. No ambiguity. No negotiation. Just a line drawn cleanly between before and after.

By the time he sleeps, the decision feels complete.

The next morning carries a different texture. Not lighter, but more deliberate. He reaches for his phone, then stops midway, aware of the movement in a way he usually isn't.

That pause feels like progress.

He gets out of bed without scrolling. The action is small, almost unimpressive, but it carries weight because it interrupts something automatic.

Through the morning, he starts noticing gaps. Waiting for coffee. Standing still. Sitting without input. Moments that were previously filled now remain open.

At first, the openness feels intentional. Like something is being reclaimed.

By afternoon, it feels less like space and more like absence.

His attention doesn't settle easily. It moves, searching for something to attach to, even when there is nothing specific it wants. Not urgency, just a low, continuous scan.

Work feels slower. Not more difficult, just less assisted. There are no quick exits between tasks, no small bursts of stimulation to reset attention.

He tells himself this is what normal is supposed to feel like.

That night, the discomfort becomes clearer. He sits longer than usual, unsure how to use the time that has opened up. The options exist, but none of them pull him in.

He tries reading. A few pages, then nothing. The words register, but they don't hold. He puts the book down and checks the time. Walks around the room. Sits again.

The absence of stimulation does not create clarity. It creates friction.

By the third day, the decision is still intact, but the feeling behind it has shifted. The urgency that made it easy to start is gone. What remains is structure without momentum.

The rules are still there. The reason feels further away.

He doesn't consciously decide to change anything. The adjustment happens quietly, through thought. YouTube isn't that bad. One video won't matter. I'll avoid the usual stuff.

Nothing about this feels like breaking the detox. It feels like refining it. That night, he opens a video. Slowly, almost carefully, as if testing whether the boundary still holds.

He watches for a minute. Then another. There's no collapse. No immediate sense of failure. Just a quiet familiarity returning. The next morning, the detox is no longer absolute. It has conditions.

This is where the shift happens. Not when discipline fails, but when definitions change. The brain does not experience this process as improvement. It experiences it as a restriction.

For days, stimulation was immediate and varied. Now it is limited, delayed, uncertain. The system doesn't interpret that as progress. It registers it as a loss.

And when something becomes restricted, its value increases.

Not because it has changed, but because access has.

Aarav doesn't think he wants to go back. He just notices that everything feels harder than expected. Starting tasks, staying with them, sitting without distraction.

He interprets that difficulty personally. As an inconsistency. As for lack of discipline.

So he tightens the rules. Less flexibility. More control. No exceptions this time. For a short while, it works. The structure sharpens again. The behavior aligns.

But the internal pressure doesn't disappear. It builds.

Each resisted impulse leaves something behind. Not enough to notice on its own, but enough to accumulate. A quiet tension that doesn't release.

By the end of the week, the detox no longer feels clean. It feels heavy.

Not because the behaviors were meaningful, but because resisting them has become constant.

He is no longer just avoiding distraction. He is holding himself in place.

That requires more energy than he expected.

On the eighth day, it gives way. Not suddenly. Not dramatically. It starts with a small shift in framing. "I'll just relax tonight."

That sentence matters. Because it doesn't feel like failure. It feels like relief.

He opens one app. Then another.

The return is immediate. Sharper than before. More engaging, more responsive. What used to feel normal now feels amplified.

This is the rebound.

After a period of restriction, stimulation hits harder. The contrast increases its impact. The same content feels more rewarding, not because it improved, but because sensitivity changed.

He doesn't stop at one video. Or two.

The restraint of the past week reverses direction. Consumption accelerates, not out of loss of control, but because the system is recalibrating.

Hours pass more quickly than usual.

By the time he stops, the detox already feels distant. Like something that belonged to a different version of the same week.

The next morning, the interpretation returns. "I need to try again." The cycle resets cleanly. Detox. Strain. Break. Rebound. Each attempt feels independent. Each failure feels personal.

But the pattern itself is consistent.

Extreme restriction creates instability. Instability makes collapse more likely. And the collapse strengthens the original behavior.

The issue is not effort. It is structured.

The detox removes behavior, but it leaves everything else untouched. The phone is still within reach. The apps are still installed. The cues still exist in the same places.

Nothing about the environment changes.

Only the rules imposed on it.

Rules require constant attention. They depend on energy, mood, and consistency. When any of those shifts, the rule weakens.

Environment does not rely on effort in the same way. It shapes behavior whether attention is present or not.

This is why the detox feels exhausting.

Not because it is difficult in theory, but because it requires continuous resistance in a system designed for ease.

Aarav begins to notice something subtle.

The detox made him more aware, but not more stable.

He can see the impulses more clearly now. He notices when they arise, how they pull, how quickly they redirect his attention.

But noticing them does not reduce them. If anything, it sharpens their presence. Awareness without adjustment creates tension.

This is where the process starts to shift away from behavior and toward identity. During the detox, Aarav thinks of himself as someone trying to quit. The identity is temporary, tied to effort.

When the effort drops, the identity disappears with it.

Nothing replaces it.

So, the system returns to what is familiar, because nothing else has been established.

Behavior follows identity more easily than it follows rules.

Rules are imposed. Identity is assumed.

Aarav doesn't frame it this way. He experiences it as inconsistency.

Some days feel controlled. Others feel automatic.

He starts questioning the method, but only slightly. Not enough to abandon it, just enough to feel uncertain. "What if this isn't working?"

The question doesn't lead to a new approach. It leads to adjustment. Shorter detox. More realistic goals. Fewer restrictions. The structure changes. The cycle remains.

Shorter attempts. Faster rebounds. Each iteration reinforces the same belief—that the solution is just one successful attempt away. But the attempt itself is part of the pattern.

The system he is using operates on extremes. Full access or full restriction. Engagement or avoidance. There is no stable middle inside that structure. So it oscillates.

Control feels temporary. Release feels inevitable.

Over time, Aarav begins to notice the transitions more than the behaviors. The shift from restraint to relief. From effort to automaticity.

The pattern becomes easier to recognize, even as it continues. This is where something changes, not in action, but in understanding.

The problem is not that he cannot sustain discipline. It is that he is trying to remove a behavior without changing the conditions that make it effortless.

The detox treats stimulation as the issue. But stimulation is not the root. It is the response. The system he exists in is built to reduce friction. Immediate access, constant availability, infinite variation.

Removing access temporarily does not change that system. It only creates a temporary gap inside it. And gaps, when held by effort alone, tend to close. What begins to emerge is a different question.

Not how to quit completely.

But how to change the way the behavior fits into the environment. Less about removal. More about placement. Less about intensity. More about structure.

The idea is less satisfying at first. It lacks the clarity of a clean break. But it carries something the detox does not.

Stability.

Aarav does not arrive at a solution immediately. Nothing resolves cleanly. But the frame begins to shift. From control to design.

From resisting impulses to understanding where they come from and how easily they are triggered. The problem starts to look less like a failure of discipline and more like a system that has been left unchanged.

And systems, unlike decisions, do not respond to intensity. They respond to structure.

Chapter 12 — Friction as Medicine

Designing Resistance Back Into Life

The phone is not on the nightstand.

Aarav notices it before he fully wakes up. His hand moves across the wood surface, slower than usual, until it reaches the empty space where the device normally rests.

For a moment, he stays still.

The absence feels small, almost irrelevant. It's not an issue; it's simply a small interruption to something that generally occurs without conscious thought.

He glances across the space.

The phone sits on the desk across the room. He left it there the night before without thinking, setting it down while clearing space beside the bed.

It’s farther than usual.

The alarm doesn’t ring.

He had set it, but the volume must have been low. Or maybe it went off and stopped. He isn’t sure.

The room is quieter than usual.

There’s no immediate input filling the space. No light from a screen, no movement, no stream of something already in progress.

He considers getting up to grab the phone.

The thought forms easily. The distance is small, just a few steps. Nothing about it is difficult.

He doesn’t get up right away.

He stays in bed a few seconds longer than usual. Not resisting. Just a pause where the next action would normally begin.

That gap stretches slightly.

It's not unpleasant. Simply unfamiliar.

When he does sit up, it seems more purposeful than it typically does. Neither lighter nor heavier—just more deliberate.

He approaches the desk and grabs the phone.

The screen in his palm illuminates, but the typical routine doesn't start right away. No automatic tapping, no immediate switch into a feed.

He checks the time first.

7:02.

Not enough to matter, but later than anticipated.

He stands there with the phone in his hand.

His thumb hovers over the screen, but nothing pulls him in. No message, no clear reason to open anything.

After a moment, he sets it back on the desk.

The motion feels incomplete, but not wrong.

In the kitchen, the routine continues as it always does. Coffee, the low hum of the machine, the same sequence of movements repeated without variation.

The phone remains in the other room.

At first, he doesn't notice.

He pours the coffee and leans against the counter.

His hand shifts slightly, as if to reach for something. Then stops. The phone isn't there.

He glances toward the other room, the absence more noticeable this time.

He considers going back for it.

Not urgently. Just as a continuation of habit.

But the moment passes.

He pours the coffee and leans against the counter. The room stays quiet longer than it usually does.

There's no background input.

No low-level engagement filling the edges of attention. Just the sound of the machine and the faint noise of the city outside.

The stillness holds.

Not comfortably. Not uncomfortably. Just there.

Across the city, Meera's phone rests beside her laptop.

The document is open, the cursor blinking steadily at the end of a paragraph she wrote the night before. She reads the last few lines, not to change them, just to reconnect with the flow.

Her hand moves toward the phone.

It's within reach. Close enough that the movement requires almost nothing. A small shift of the wrist, a glance downward.

She unlocks it without thinking.

A notification opens into a video. Then another follows. The transition is seamless, requiring no decision, no pause.

The document remains open.

But it recedes slightly.

When she looks back at it, the starting point feels less immediate than it did a moment ago. Not difficult, just further away.

She tells herself she'll begin in a minute.

The minute stretches.

Back in the kitchen, Aarav finishes his coffee.

The phone is still in the other room.

He notices the difference again, but this time it feels less like absence and more like delay. The impulse appears, but it doesn't resolve instantly.

There's a space between wanting and doing.

He walks back to the desk and checks the phone briefly. A few notifications. Nothing urgent.

He unlocks it, scrolls once, then stops.

The movement feels slightly less automatic than it did the day before.

Not controlled.

Just interrupted.

This is the part that usually goes unnoticed.
Not the behavior itself, but how quickly it begins.

A thought appears, and the action follows almost immediately. There's barely any space between them.

When that distance increases, even slightly, something changes. Not dramatically, but enough to slow the sequence.

That small interruption is friction. It doesn't feel like effort or resistance. It shows up as a bit of distance—a delay that makes the next step less immediate.

The system responds to that difference. Not consciously. But reliably. When access is immediate, behavior accelerates. When access is delayed, behavior softens.

The impulse still appears. But it has somewhere to go before it becomes action. That space matters more than it seems. Later that afternoon, Aarav sits at his desk.

His laptop is open. A task waits on the screen. Nothing complex, nothing unfamiliar.

His phone rests a few feet away.

Close enough to reach. Far enough to require movement.

He begins working.

A few minutes pass before the impulse appears. A brief urge to check something, not specific, just a shift in attention looking for relief.

His hand moves slightly. Then stops. The phone is not within immediate reach. The movement would require leaning forward. A small adjustment. Nothing significant.

But enough. The pause extends. The urge weakens slightly. He returns to the screen. The task continues. Not smoothly. Not perfectly. But without interruption.

Later that evening, Aarav sits on the couch, the day winding down around him.

The urge to check his phone returns, softer this time. Not tied to anything specific. Just a familiar pull toward something easy.

The phone is still on the desk in the other room.

He considers getting up to get it. The distance is small. Familiar.

For a moment, he stays where he is. The impulse lingers, then shifts. Not gone, just less immediate.

He could get up and scroll. Or he could stay.

This time, the choice is visible.

Across the city, Meera's phone lights up again.

She picks it up before the thought fully forms. The action is clean, uninterrupted, practiced.

The document remains open.

Unfinished.

Neither of them notices the difference as a principle. Aarav has begun to introduce small amounts of distance without fully realizing it.

Meera hasn't. Her environment still allows each impulse to turn into action without interruption.

They experience it as a mood. As a focus. As an inconsistency. But the structure underneath is simple.

One environment removes distance. The other introduces it. And behavior adjusts accordingly. Friction does not eliminate desire. It changes its path.

When something requires nothing, it becomes difficult to refuse. Not because it is meaningful. But because it is immediate.

When something requires a step, a shift, a delay, it becomes easier to ignore. Not because it is unimportant. But because it is no longer automatic. This is where the difference begins.

Not in discipline. Not in intention. In structure.

The systems surrounding behavior determine how easily it unfolds. When those systems remove all resistance, action follows impulse without interruption.

When they introduce even small barriers, the sequence changes. Impulse meets space. Space allows choice.

Not always. Not perfectly. But more often than before. This is why removing behavior entirely feels unstable. It relies on constant effort.

Constant awareness. Constant resistance.

Friction does not require the same level of attention. It operates quietly. In the background. Shaping behavior without demanding control.

By evening, Aarav notices something he wouldn't have named before. The day did not feel lighter. But it felt slightly less fragmented.

The transitions between tasks were slower. But also less scattered. He still checked his phone. Still moved between things.

Nothing was eliminated. But something was reduced. Not the behavior itself. The speed at which it took over. That difference is easy to miss.

It does not feel like progress. It feels like less interference. And that is enough. The problem was never access.

It was how little stood between intention and action.

When that distance disappears, behavior becomes automatic. When it returns, even slightly, something else becomes possible.

Not control. Not discipline. Just a moment.

And sometimes, that moment is all that's needed to change what happens next.

Aarav sits at his desk, the phone a few feet away.

It lights up briefly, then goes still.

He glances at it, then back to the screen in front of him.

This time, he doesn't reach for it.

Chapter 13 — The Reset Protocol

Effort Before Reward

There is no notice when morning arrives. The room is still dark, silent, and free of artificial disturbances.

Aarav wakes slowly into it, his eyes adjusting without urgency. Nothing occurs for a few seconds. The pause lasts longer than normal.

His hand drifts slightly across the mattress, the old reflex starting to form, then stopping before it fully lands. The urge passes without resolving into action.

In the kitchen, the sequence continues without interruption. Water, coffee grinds, the machine's soft hum—each step comes after the other without being divided.

He thinks about his phone once. The impulse rises, then fades before it turns into movement.

But the moment passes before it turns into action. He leans against the counter instead, waiting as the coffee finishes brewing.

Steam rises and fades in the quiet space. Nothing fills the gap, and for once, nothing needs to.

He takes the first sip and stands there a little longer than usual. The taste registers clearly, not stronger, just less diluted by distraction.

There is no shift in mood, no sudden clarity. Just a morning that begins without interruption.

He gets dressed without pausing between actions. The sequence moves forward without small detours breaking it apart.

On his way out, he checks his phone. Just a quick glance at the screen. Notifications wait as they always do, unchanged and immediate.

He looks at them briefly, then locks the screen again. The order has already changed despite the little action.

Outside, the city moves as it always does, but he passes through it without picking anything up along the way.

Across the city, Meera sits at her desk with her laptop open but untouched. The cursor blinks at the top of an empty page while her phone rests beside her, screen dark for once.

The impulse to check it appears almost immediately. A small reflex at the edge of attention, familiar enough to feel automatic.

Her hand moves toward it, then pauses. Not deliberately. The movement simply slows long enough for the thought to pass.

She turns back to the screen instead. The first sentence comes slowly, but it comes before anything else does.

On the train, people stand and sit in quiet patterns of motion. Screens light up across the compartment, each one holding a separate stream.

Aarav notices the reflex to reach into his pocket. The impulse rises, then stalls before turning into action.

He lets his hand rest instead. The movement fades on its own.

The ride feels longer than usual, even though nothing's changed. Without the usual noise, the gaps between moments stand out more.

He watches them instead of filling them. The experience feels slower, but also more continuous.

At work, the shift becomes more visible in how things begin. He sits down, opens his laptop, and starts without a prelude.

There is no quick check, no small delay to ease into the task. The work doesn't feel easier, but it begins sooner.

A few minutes pass before the first impulse appears. It's vague, not tied to anything specific, just a pull away from what he's doing.

His hand shifts slightly toward his phone, then pauses. The interruption is small, but it breaks the automatic sequence.

The urge remains, but it weakens slightly when it doesn't resolve immediately. He returns to the screen, and the task continues.

Ten minutes pass without interruption. Then fifteen.

The work itself hasn't changed, but the entry into it has. Starting earlier changes how long he stays.

A notification appears in the corner of the screen. The familiar flicker of curiosity follows almost instantly.

He glances at it, then back at the document. The delay is brief, but enough to interrupt the reflex.

The notification fades without being opened. The moment closes without expanding into something else.

Around midday, the old sequence returns without warning. He unlocks his phone and slips into a stream of videos.

The pace picks up quickly—familiar, automatic. One clip replaces another, then another. The pull feels stronger than it did in the morning.

He tells himself it'll just be a minute.

It isn't.

Time stretches without markers. Five minutes pass, then ten. The movement is smooth, continuous, hard to interrupt.

Somewhere in the middle of it, he becomes aware of what's happening. Not after the fact—during it.

The recognition doesn't stop it immediately.

His thumb keeps moving. Another video starts. Then another.

There's a brief tension now—two directions at once. Continue, or stop.

"One more" comes first.

Then again.

The loop holds longer than he intends.

When he finally stops, it isn't clean. There's a slight resistance in the movement as he locks the screen and sets the phone down.

He sits there for a moment, aware that the pattern didn't break easily this time.

Then the pause returns—unsteady, but enough.

He turns back to his work, not with momentum, but with intention.

He locks the screen and places the phone down. The interruption ends without turning into a longer spiral.

He sits there for a moment, not immediately returning to work. The pause holds without being filled.

Then he continues.

That gap—small, unforced—changes the transition back. It feels less like recovery and more like continuation.

Meera notices the pattern later that afternoon while answering emails. Every few minutes, her attention drifts toward something else before the thought fully finishes.

Normally, she would follow it automatically. A quick check. A short scroll. Something small enough not to register as interruption.

This time, she notices the shift earlier. The impulse still appears, but it no longer feels invisible while it's happening.

She stays with the task a little longer than usual. Not focused exactly, just less divided.

Later in the afternoon, he goes to the gym as usual. The environment remains unchanged, familiar in its structure and rhythm.

What changes is what comes before and between the movements. There is no pre-stimulation filling the space.

No scrolling between sets, no background input running quietly. Each segment of effort stands on its own.

At first, the pace feels slightly off. The gaps between actions are more visible than before.

He finishes a set and sits down without reaching for anything. The stillness stretches longer than expected.

The urge to fill it appears, then softens. The moment holds without needing to be replaced.

By the third set, the rhythm stabilizes. Movement and rest begin to connect more directly.

The session feels slower, but also less fragmented. Each part follows from the last without interruption.

After the workout, he walks home without headphones. The city noise replaces the usual curated input.

Cars pass, conversations overlap, footsteps echo along the pavement. The sound isn't controlled, but it doesn't need to be.

Later in the evening, he picks up his phone and slips into scrolling again. This time, it goes deeper.

One video turns into several. The pace builds quickly—familiar, immersive. For a while, there's no interruption. Just continuous movement from one clip to the next.

Then the contrast appears. Not after he stops—while he's still in it. The shift is subtle at first. A small awareness running alongside the motion.

His thumb slows, but doesn't stop. Another video plays. Then it hesitates.

The pull is still there, but weaker now—just enough space for the sequence to break. He locks the screen and sets the phone aside.

The stop isn't forced, but it isn't effortless either. He sits in the quiet that follows. This time, it holds.

This is where the shift becomes clear.

For a long time, reward came first. It opened the day, filled the gaps, and shaped everything that followed. Effort had to compete with that pattern, starting only after stimulation had already taken its place.

Now the order has quietly reversed.

Effort comes first. Reward follows.

Nothing has been removed. The same distractions are still available, just no longer leading the sequence.

That small change alters how the system responds. Anticipation begins to return—not as intensity, but as steady engagement. Tasks don't become exciting, but they stop feeling completely flat.

Action starts sooner. It holds longer.

Even when the pattern breaks, it doesn't collapse. It bends, then resets.

Aarav doesn't think of it in these terms. He notices it in simpler ways—how things begin, how long they continue, and how easily they restart.

Even when he slips, the pattern doesn't collapse entirely. It bends, then returns. He closes the screen, but this time it isn't a reaction—it's a choice.

Not immediate. Not clean. But deliberate. He knew where it was going, and let it play out longer than he needed to.

That's new. The awareness arrives earlier now, sometimes before the action fully takes over.

Not to stop it instantly, but to make it visible. He sits in the quiet for a moment, not analyzing it, just noticing the difference.

The pattern isn't gone. It's just no longer invisible.

That evening, Meera returns to a document she had abandoned earlier in the week. Normally, restarting would feel heavier than the work itself.

Tonight, the resistance is still there, but smaller. She rereads the last paragraph, adjusts a sentence, then keeps going without breaking the flow to check something else.

The difference is subtle enough to miss if she wasn't paying attention. The work doesn't feel exciting. It just holds a little longer before her attention slips away.

For now, that's enough.

Later that night, he sits at his desk again.

Not to check anything. Not to switch tasks. Just to continue.

The screen lights up. The document opens where he left it.

For a moment, nothing happens.

No pull. No competing impulse running underneath.

Just the next step.

He starts.

The work moves forward without interruption. One line into the next, then another. No breaks to reset, no drifting away and returning.

Time passes, but it doesn't fragment.

At some point, he notices the absence of resistance—not as something dramatic, just as something no longer there.

The work finishes where it was meant to.

He stops, not because something pulled him away, but because there is nothing left to continue. The screen stays open for a moment longer. Then he closes it.

No impulse follows. He sits there briefly, in the quiet that remains. This time, it isn't something he's holding. It holds on its own. Effort came first.

And this time, it carried all the way through.

Chapter 14 — Relearning Focus

The Return of Depth

Aarav opens the research draft he has avoided for the past six days.

The document is dense with unfinished arguments, highlighted contradictions, and scattered notes that no longer make immediate sense. Several sections challenge the core conclusion he thought he had already settled. To finish it, he will need to compare competing ideas, restructure entire sections, and think carefully enough to notice where the logic breaks.

He has delayed working on it repeatedly.

Each time he opened the file earlier in the week, his attention drifted almost immediately toward easier things—emails, short videos, reorganizing notes, anything that created movement without requiring sustained thought. The work demanded too much uninterrupted attention to enter casually.

Now the document sits open in front of him again.

For a moment, he just looks at it.

The resistance appears almost instantly. Not dramatic enough to stop him completely, but heavy enough to make the beginning feel unpleasant. His attention pushes outward at the edges, already searching for somewhere easier to go.

Still, he starts.

The first several minutes feel disorganized and slow. He rereads the same paragraph multiple times without fully processing it. One sentence leads to another, but nothing connects cleanly yet. His attention keeps loosening before ideas can fully develop.

Several times, the impulse to leave appears.

Check something else.

Open another tab.

Come back later when your mind feels clearer.

The thoughts arrive automatically, almost faster than the work itself. The task still feels mentally abrasive, like his attention hasn't settled deeply enough to hold the complexity in front of him.

But he stays anyway.

Nothing clicks at first. The work remains effortful. Progress is uneven. He adjusts the same paragraph repeatedly and questions whether he is thinking clearly enough to continue.

Still, he does not leave.

Gradually, the resistance stops dominating his attention. Not all at once, and not dramatically. His focus simply remains in place long enough for the ideas to begin connecting.

At some point, the resistance stops being the most noticeable thing. He doesn't mark the shift when it happens, and there's no clear transition. His attention just settles enough to hold.

At first, the change is difficult to notice.

The resistance is still present, but it no longer interrupts every few seconds. His attention remains with the material long enough for individual ideas to stop feeling disconnected from one another.

A paragraph that felt opaque earlier begins to organize itself.

He notices an assumption buried beneath one of his arguments and restructures the section around it. Then another contradiction surfaces—smaller this time, but clearer than before. Instead of losing momentum when he encounters the problem, his attention stays with it long enough to work through it.

That is new.

Earlier in the day, each difficult section felt like friction. Now the complexity begins to feel workable. Not easier, exactly, but stable enough to remain inside without immediately reaching for escape.

He rereads fewer lines.

His thoughts begin extending further before breaking apart. One idea carries into the next without requiring him to consciously restart his attention each time.

Minutes pass without him checking anything else.

The work starts absorbing more of his awareness. Background distractions lose definition at the edges. The room remains there physically, but less of his attention keeps returning to it.

Another section clicks into place.

Then another.

He adjusts a sequence of ideas that had felt unresolved for days and suddenly sees how they connect. The insight arrives gradually rather than dramatically, but once it appears, the structure feels obvious enough that he wonders why he couldn't hold it together earlier.

His attention settles deeper.

Not forced. Not tightly controlled.

Just continuous.

The effort behind remaining focused becomes less visible to him because less of his attention is being spent resisting the work itself.

One thought leads directly into another.

The material begins pulling him forward faster than distraction can interrupt him.

Time changes inside that continuity. It no longer breaks into small, separate pieces. It stretches without interruption.

The progression of thought becomes difficult to separate into individual steps.

He moves through one problem, then directly into the next, without noticing the transitions between them. Earlier, each difficult section forced him to stop and rebuild his attention from the beginning. Now the continuity holds long enough for the work itself to carry him forward.

The material becomes more coherent as he stays with it.

Connections that previously felt too complex to hold at once begin fitting together inside the same stretch of attention. He compares ideas across multiple sections without losing the thread midway through. Arguments that felt fragmented earlier now remain stable long enough to examine properly.

At some point, he stops noticing the effort involved.

His attention narrows naturally around the work. The urge to check something else still appears occasionally, but it fades before fully forming into action. Once, a notification briefly lights his phone screen beside him. His eyes shift toward it automatically, then return to the document almost immediately.

The interruption doesn't break the continuity.

That surprises him more than anything else.

Earlier, even small distractions would have scattered his attention completely. Now the thread remains intact underneath them.

The work deepens further.

A section he had postponed rewriting for nearly a week finally becomes clear enough to resolve. He rearranges several ideas, cuts unnecessary explanations, and feels the structure tighten into something more precise. For the first time in days, the work feels like it is moving somewhere instead of resisting him at every step.

Only after finishing the section does he lean back slightly in his chair.

The room feels strangely still.

He glances toward the television across the room, then toward the clock.

An hour and twelve minutes have passed.

The number feels unfamiliar more than impressive.

He tries to remember the last moment he consciously resisted the work and cannot find it clearly. At some point, the effort of staying had dissolved into the experience of continuing.

And underneath that realization, something else becomes clear.

This was the missing condition.

Not motivation.

Not discipline.

Sustained depth.

Without enough uninterrupted attention, nothing had remained in place long enough to fully develop.

He sits there for a moment without reaching for anything else. The pause holds on its own without collapsing into distraction. Then he turns back and continues.

The second stretch begins with less hesitation. The distance between starting and continuing has shortened. He doesn't need to convince himself again.

The work resumes where it left off. There is no reset, no need to rebuild context. The thread is still intact.

A thought appears midway through the task. It's familiar and quiet, almost automatic in tone. Check your phone.

His hand shifts slightly in response. The phone is within reach, and nothing is stopping him. The action would take almost no effort.

But the sequence isn't complete. The thought lingers for a moment, then softens. He returns to the screen.

The interruption dissolves before it becomes behavior. The impulse remains what it is—just a suggestion. It no longer guarantees movement.

This is where the difference becomes visible. The impulses still appear, unchanged in form. What changes is what follows them.

They don't always turn into action. And when they don't, something else has space to continue. The work deepens quietly.

What felt flat at the beginning begins to shift. Not into excitement, but into something steadier. A kind of engagement that wasn't available earlier.

He stops noticing the effort behind each step. The task begins to organize itself as he moves through it. One idea leads to another without force.

He doesn't need to reread the same lines repeatedly. He doesn't lose track of where he is. The continuity holds.

This was the missing piece before. Not ability, not knowledge, just the capacity to remain. Without that, nothing had time to develop.

Earlier, attention would reset before anything could take shape. Now it stays long enough for structure to form. That changes everything about the experience.

He finishes a section and pauses naturally. The pause doesn't pull him away from the task. It sits there without demanding replacement.

He continues without needing a reset. The transition feels direct and unforced. There is less negotiation between actions.

That reduction is subtle but consistent. Starting feels lighter, and continuing feels easier. Stopping no longer triggers immediate escape.

By evening, something subtle becomes clear. There is less hesitation before beginning tasks. The internal negotiation has quieted.

He notices it again later that night when he returns briefly to finish another section.

The work resumes faster than it would have earlier in the week. His attention settles with less resistance, and the familiar impulses to leave no longer carry the same authority they once did.

They still appear occasionally.

But they no longer define the direction of his attention.

Later that evening, Meera pulls a book from the corner of her shelf.

A folded receipt still marks the place where she stopped reading nearly three months earlier.

She remembers intending to continue it several different times. Usually she would read two or three pages before her attention drifted elsewhere. The experience had slowly changed from immersion into maintenance—reading enough to feel like she was still someone who read.

She sits near the window and opens to the marked page.

At first, the words feel distant.

She reads a paragraph, then realizes she has absorbed almost none of it. Her attention pulls outward automatically, searching for something faster, lighter, easier to enter. For a moment, she considers setting the book back down.

Instead, she keeps reading.

The first chapter moves slowly. Not because the writing lacks momentum, but because her attention still resists remaining in one place long enough to fully enter it.

Gradually, that resistance weakens.

The sentences begin holding together across longer stretches of thought. Details stop disappearing immediately after she reads them. The atmosphere of the book becomes easier to remain inside without mentally leaving every few moments.

By the second chapter, something changes.

Her attention settles deeply enough that the movement of reading becomes continuous. She no longer feels herself repeatedly returning to the page. The narrative carries forward on its own.

The room around her softens at the edges.

Time stops dividing itself into noticeable fragments. Pages pass without her tracking them carefully. Characters who had initially felt distant begin feeling emotionally present in a way she hasn't experienced for a long time.

At some point, she realizes she hasn't checked her phone once.

That realization feels strangely unfamiliar.

She glances down near the bottom of the page and notices the page number.

One hundred and forty-three.

She blinks, briefly disoriented by the distance.

Earlier that month, reading ten pages had felt difficult. Now entire sections have passed without interruption. The experience feels less like forcing concentration and more like finally remaining somewhere long enough for depth to emerge naturally.

When she finally closes the book, the silence in the room feels full instead of empty.

For a moment, she simply sits there holding it.

Not because she is trying to preserve the experience.

Because she has not felt that kind of uninterrupted presence in a very long time.

This repeats in small ways throughout the evening. He doesn't always stay. But he leaves less often than before. And when he leaves, he returns sooner.

Something begins to change underneath that pattern. Not in what he does, but in what he expects from himself. The assumption starts to shift.

Each time he remains, even briefly, it reinforces something quiet. The expectation that he will leave weakens. The expectation that he can stay grows.

He doesn't describe it as confidence. It doesn't feel like a belief he chose. It feels like less doubt at the start of things.

The question of whether he will follow through appears less often. That absence reduces friction. Starting becomes simpler.

Later that night, Aarav reopens the document one final time before shutting down for the evening. He scrolls slowly through the sections he worked on earlier.

The structure holds together now.

Arguments that had felt fragmented and unstable a week ago move in a clear direction. Several ideas that once competed against each other now connect naturally across the same line of thought. Even the sections he rewrote most heavily no longer feel forced into coherence. They actually developed.

He pauses at one paragraph and reads it again carefully. Not because he doubts it. Because he recognizes the level of thinking it requires.

A few weeks earlier, he would not have remained with the work long enough to reach this point. His attention would have fractured long before the ideas had time to stabilize into something complete.

Now the depth remained long enough for the work to become meaningful.

That realization stays with him quietly. Across the apartment, Meera sits with her book resting closed in her lap. Neither of them says much for a while.

The silence feels different from the kind that usually follows exhaustion or distraction. It feels settled. Continuous. Like something in the background has stopped pulling at them every few seconds.

Meera runs her thumb along the edge of the pages. "I forgot reading could feel like that," she says softly. Aarav looks toward her.

He understands exactly what she means. Not because they both concentrated harder. Because they remained somewhere long enough for depth to return.

For months, their attention had existed in fragments too brief to fully hold anything difficult, absorbing, or meaningful. Everything was interrupted before it had time to deepen.

Now that continuity has started returning. Not perfectly. Not permanently. But enough to recognize the difference. Aarav closes the laptop gently.

For a moment, neither of them reaches for anything else. The quiet no longer feels empty. It feels inhabited.

Chapter 15 — Discipline Without Harshness

Dependability Above Intensity

The alarm sounds at 6:30.

While asleep, Aarav hears it faintly. He reaches for the nightstand, and silences it without fully waking up. The space remains black.

Usually, he gets up within a few minutes now. The sequence has become more familiar over the past several weeks—water, coffee, movement, work before distraction. Not perfectly consistent, but stable enough to begin without much negotiation.

He shut his eyes once again this morning.

Sunlight is already peeking through the drapes as he awakens a second time.

9:14.

For a moment, he stays still. The realization arrives almost immediately. The missed morning. The broken sequence. The delay.

His body reacts before his thoughts fully organize. A small tightening across his chest. The familiar sensation of having already drifted too far from the day to recover it properly.

Earlier, that feeling would have spread quickly.

The logic was always immediate once the pattern broke. You already missed the morning. The structure's gone now. Start again tomorrow.

The thought still appears now, almost unchanged in tone. But something about it feels less convincing than it used to.

He lies there a moment longer, watching the thought continue without immediately following it. The room remains quiet.

Nothing dramatic happens inside him. No surge of discipline. No sudden correction.

Just a pause long enough for the sequence to stop accelerating.

He sits up slowly.

The day already feels less organized than usual. The rhythm he had started building over the past few weeks is missing its normal beginning. The absence is noticeable immediately.

In the kitchen, the motions feel slightly disconnected. Coffee grinds. Running water. The low mechanical hum of the machine.

The sequence still happens, but without the same continuity underneath it.

His phone rests beside the counter. The impulse appears almost automatically now. If the structure is already broken, some part of him wants the familiar relief that usually follows.

A quick scroll.

Something easy. Something that removes the feeling of being behind.

He unlocks the screen.

A notification opens into another. Then another. The movement begins smoothly, familiar in its pacing. Headlines. Messages. Short videos sliding upward beneath his thumb.

Ten minutes pass.

Then fifteen.

The old feeling begins returning quietly underneath the scrolling—not pleasure exactly, but disengagement. A gradual loosening of attention.

Earlier, this is where the pattern usually deepened. The morning would disappear first. Then the afternoon would soften around it. One interruption becomes permission for another.

The structure wouldn't just bend. It would collapse completely. His thumb slows slightly.

The awareness appears while the behavior is still happening. Not afterward. During it. That difference remains small, but noticeable.

He watches another video begin loading automatically. The sound starts before he fully registers what it is.

Then he locks the screen.

The stop feels incomplete. Part of him still wants to continue. The momentum hasn't disappeared. The pull remains active underneath the interruption.

But the sequence has broken enough for another choice to become visible. He stands there quietly for a moment. The morning still feels off. Nothing has reset.

But the damage no longer feels total.

Later that afternoon, Aarav sits at his desk staring at the unfinished section of his research draft.

The resistance feels stronger than it did the previous evening. His attention still carries some of the looseness from the morning. Thoughts drift more easily. The entry into the work feels heavier again.

For several minutes, he adjusts small things around the document without actually beginning. Resize the window. Reread old notes. Check the formatting.

The familiar avoidance appears in quieter forms first.

He notices it gradually.

Earlier, noticing the drift would have sharpened the self-monitoring around it. Focus. Stop wasting time. Just start.

The internal pressure usually increased the friction instead of reducing it. Attention tightened around performance rather than the work itself.

Now the reaction feels less aggressive. He notices the avoidance without immediately turning it into judgment. The resistance remains.

But it no longer multiplies. After a while, he begins anyway.

The first few paragraphs move slowly. His attention still slips occasionally toward easier things. Twice, he reaches for his phone before stopping midway through the movement.

The impulses haven't disappeared. Neither has distraction.

But the interruptions recover faster now.

Across the city, Meera sits cross-legged on the couch with her laptop open beside her.

An unfinished article waits on the screen. She had planned to finish it the night before, but halfway through writing, her attention scattered into smaller distractions—messages, videos, reorganizing tabs, reading things she didn't need.

Eventually she closed the laptop without finishing anything.

This morning, the unfinished document still carries the emotional residue of that experience. The resistance begins before she even opens it fully.

Not because the work itself feels impossible.

Because restarting means reconnecting with the feeling that she had drifted away from it again.

Earlier, this is where the spiral usually deepened. The delay would become self-criticism. The self-criticism would make reentry feel heavier.

Then avoidance would grow around the weight of returning. The cycle often lasted longer than the original interruption itself.

She opens the document carefully. The unfinished paragraph waits near the bottom of the page. For a few moments, she just looks at it.

The discomfort appears immediately—not dramatic, just enough to create hesitation. A familiar thought moves quietly underneath it. You keep doing this.

The sentence lands softer than it once did. Not because she fully believes otherwise. Because she no longer follows the thought as far.

That distance matters. She rereads the paragraph once. Then adjust a sentence. Then another.

The movement feels uneven at first. Her attention still drifts occasionally toward her phone beside her. Twice, she unlocks it without fully realizing she has done it.

But each interruption ends sooner.

Meera notices this later that evening while rereading sections of the article she finally finished.

The work is not perfect. Several paragraphs still feel weaker than she wanted. A section near the middle needs restructuring. Another argument feels underdeveloped.

Normally, she would continue adjusting the draft long past the point of usefulness, trying to remove the discomfort completely before allowing herself to stop.

Tonight, the tension feels lighter.

Incomplete does not automatically feel unacceptable anymore.

She closes the laptop.

The unfinished parts remain unfinished. But they no longer follow her emotionally through the rest of the evening.

Later that night, Aarav glances briefly toward the phone charging across the room.

The thought appears automatically. A few videos before sleep.

For a moment, he considers it. Then the thought passes without becoming action.

By night, the missed morning no longer feels significant. Not because it didn't matter.

Because it remained one part of the day instead of spreading across all of it. The continuity held. Imperfectly. But enough.

Aarav turns off the light and lies back against the pillow. The room settles gradually around him. Tomorrow no longer feels like a restart. Just a continuation.

Chapter 16 — From Stimulation to Direction

The Anchor's Purpose

The flat is silent save for the faint sound of typing. Aarav is sitting at the dining table with several printed documents scattered beside his laptop, some heavily marked, others untouched.

The evening light outside gradually illuminates the windows. He reads the same passage again, modifies a sentence, and keeps on. The motion seems stable—it's not quick or easy, but it's steady enough to grip.

Several months ago, work like this rarely lasted long. Attention would loosen quickly, and a difficult section would create pressure almost immediately. One interruption usually opened into several more, until the original thread disappeared completely beneath smaller distractions.

Now the interruptions arrive differently.

A thought appears briefly. Check your phone. The impulse rises automatically, but something underneath it has changed. The urge no longer feels urgent enough to reorganize his attention around it.

He keeps reading.

The paragraph sharpens gradually as he stays with it. One idea leads into another without requiring him to consciously force the transition. The continuity holds long enough for the work itself to carry him forward.

Across the room, his phone lights up once against the dark counter, then goes still again. He doesn't notice.

Later that evening, Aarav closes the laptop and leans back slightly in his chair. The work is unfinished, and several sections still need revision. One argument remains unstable near the middle, unresolved in a way that would have bothered him deeply before.

Earlier, unfinished effort followed him everywhere. It stayed active in the background, quietly draining attention even while he escaped into easier forms of relief. The discomfort rarely came from the work itself. It came from knowing he kept leaving it.

Now the relationship feels different.

The work remains open, but not emotionally scattered in the same way. He knows where he is returning tomorrow, and that certainty changes something subtle underneath the surface.

Not emotionally. Structurally.

Across the city, Meera walks slowly through a bookstore near her apartment. Rain taps lightly against the front windows while quiet music moves through the background. A few people wander between shelves without urgency.

She stops near a table stacked with essay collections and flips through one absentmindedly. Earlier, spaces like this often felt difficult to remain inside fully. Her attention would fracture almost immediately, and silence created restlessness faster than interest could deepen into engagement.

Now the experience unfolds differently.

She reads several pages standing there without noticing time pass in separate pieces. The words hold long enough to become immersive rather than informational. A sentence catches her attention and stays there after she closes the book.

Not because it is profound.

Because her mind remained with it long enough for it to register completely.

She places the book back carefully and continues walking through the aisles. Around her, nothing dramatic changes. People browse shelves, someone coughs softly near the back, and rain continues pressing lightly against the glass.

But the environment no longer feels like something to move through quickly on the way toward more stimulation. It feels inhabitable.

Later that night, Aarav stands at the kitchen counter rinsing a coffee mug while Meera sits nearby reading quietly, one leg folded beneath her. The apartment remains dim except for the small light above the stove.

Neither of them says much. The silence moves naturally between small sounds—the running water, a page turning, traffic passing faintly below the building.

Earlier, silence often created invisible pressure. One of them would reach for a screen almost automatically, and conversation became thinner around distraction, repeatedly interrupted before it could deepen into anything sustained.

Now the pauses remain intact longer.

Not because they are trying to protect them. Because neither feels the same urgency to escape them anymore.

Aarav dries the mug and sets it beside the sink. “I think I’m going to continue the research project,” he says after a while.

Meera looks up from the book. “The same one?”

He nods slightly. “There’s still a lot missing.”

“That’s probably why you like it.”

A faint smile appears briefly across his face. The answer settles quietly between them, carrying more certainty than excitement.

Not ambition exactly. Something steadier.

The work matters even when the feeling changes around it. Direction without requiring constant excitement.

Near midnight, Meera closes her book and rests her head lightly against the couch. Aarav sits across from her with a notebook open beside him, adjusting a few handwritten notes from earlier.

Neither of them appears especially productive. Neither appears entertained. Still, the atmosphere feels full in a way that would have seemed strange months earlier.

Nothing dramatic is happening.

No constant input. No background stream competing for attention every few seconds. Just an uninterrupted presence stretched across an ordinary evening.

Outside, rain continues softly against the windows. Aarav glances briefly toward the phone resting untouched on the counter.

The screen remains dark.

For a moment, he tries remembering the last time silence felt impossible to sit inside. The memory feels distant now—not erased, just less familiar.

He looks back down at the notebook. Then he continues writing.

Conclusion

Awake, Not Ascetic

The apartment is quiet except for rain tapping softly against the windows. Meera sits on the couch with a book open in her lap, one leg folded beneath her. Across from her, Aarav leans forward slightly at the table, pen moving slowly across a page of handwritten notes.

Neither of them has spoken in the last twenty minutes.

The silence doesn't feel empty. It moves naturally around them—rain against glass, a page turning, the faint sound of traffic several floors below. Small sounds that used to disappear beneath constant background noise now arrive clearly, unhurried.

Meera reads the same paragraph twice, not because she lost focus, but because something in the sentence holds her attention long enough to return to it. The words settle differently the second time—less hurried, more complete. She can feel herself inside the reading rather than moving across its surface.

Earlier, moments like this rarely lasted. Her attention would fracture before depth could develop. A notification. A thought about something else. The quiet pressure to fill silence before it became uncomfortable. One small interruption usually opened into several more, until presence dissolved completely into distraction.

Now the continuity holds.

Across the room, Aarav pauses mid-sentence, thinking. His phone rests on the counter several feet away, screen dark. A few months ago, he would've reached for it without thinking—just to check, just briefly, just in case something needed immediate attention.

The urge still appears.

Check it out.

The impulse rises automatically.

Then it passes.

He returns to the sentence, finishes it, and continues writing.

Nothing about the evening looks remarkable from the outside. No breakthrough. No dramatic transformation. Just two people remaining fully inside an ordinary moment long enough for it to feel complete.

Thought breaks apart before it deepens. Conversations thin out beneath divided attention. Effort becomes harder to sustain once novelty fades. Days begin moving faster while feeling strangely less inhabited at the same time.

Most people experience these changes personally, even when the source remains difficult to name.

They feel it while staring at unfinished work they cannot seem to begin properly. They feel it during conversations repeatedly interrupted by invisible urges to check something else. They feel it at night when exhaustion exists beside restlessness instead of replacing it.

Not because something is wrong with them.

Because attention adapts to its environment, whether that adaptation is helpful or not.

An hour later, Aarav stands and stretches slightly, setting the pen down beside his notebook. He walks to the kitchen and pours himself a glass of water.

Neither asks what the other is doing. The atmosphere does not require constant interaction to remain connected.

He looks briefly toward the phone resting near the sink. The screen remains dark.

For a moment, he realizes he's gone several hours without thinking about it.
The recognition passes quietly—not as achievement, just as contrast.
Earlier, attention moved toward stimulation with the same automatic consistency as breathing. Most impulses completed themselves before awareness entered the process.
Now the sequence slows often enough to become visible while it's still unfolding.
That visibility matters. Once awareness enters the pattern, distraction stops feeling completely unconscious. The

behavior may still happen, but it no longer carries the same invisibility it once did.

That is why awareness changes people more reliably than shame.

Shame turns every mistake into evidence of failure. Awareness simply allows patterns to become recognizable before they fully take over. One creates exhaustion. The other creates choice.

Not perfectly.

But enough.

Outside, the rain begins slowing against the windows. Meera closes the notebook and leans back slightly in her chair while Aarav stands quietly near the counter finishing his water.

Nothing about the moment appears especially meaningful from the outside.

No breakthrough. No dramatic transformation. No final declaration about becoming a different person.

Just two people existing inside an ordinary evening without needing to escape it every few seconds.

For a long time, unconscious stimulation shaped attention so completely that stillness began feeling empty by comparison. Now the emptiness is gone.

Not because life suddenly became more exciting.

Because attention remained present long enough for ordinary experience to regain depth again.

Aarav sets the glass beside the sink and turns off the kitchen light. The apartment settles softly into darkness around them as the rain fades somewhere beyond the windows.

His phone remains where it is. This time, he leaves it there without thinking about it twice.

Verses Kindler Publication

Verses Kindler Publication

Reach us through our website -
https://www.verseskindlerpublication.com/
For more information visit our
Instagram or Facebook page.

www.ingramcontent.com/pod-product-compliance
Lightning Source LLC
LaVergne TN
LVHW010720061126
851857LV00014B/1271
9788169248143